HOW CAN YOU BUY

A BUSINESS WITHOUT

OVERPAYING

HOW CAN YOU BUY
A BUSINESS
WITHOUT OVERPAYING

More Money Left On
Your Side Of The Table

by Eugene Merfeld and Gary L. Schine

THE CONSULTANT PRESS
New York, New York

PUBLISHED BY:

THE CONSULTANT PRESS
163 AMSTERDAM AVENUE
NEW YORK, NEW YORK 10023

(212) 838-8640

Susan P. Levy, Editor

ISBN 0-913069-29-9

Library of Congress Catalog Card Number 91-073308

Printed and bound in the United States Of America

see card

Publisher's - Cataloging in Publication

Schine, Gary L., 1951-
    How you can buy a business without overpaying: more money left on your side of the table/ by Gary L. Schine, Eugene Merfeld
    p. cm.   ; 28 cm.
    143 p
    Includes bibliographic references and index.
    ISBN 0-913069-29-9 (pbk.)

1. Business enterprises, Purchasing. I. Merfeld, Eugene, 1930 II. Title

HD2341 1991   338.71
                                700 10

Table Of Contents

The *Gender Neutral* Issue

Unfortunately, the English language does not provide a non-sexist solution to the use of the pronouns *he* and *she*. Traditionally, of course, *he* was used to mean *he* and *she* when not referring to a specific person. Like so many writers, we have been frustrated in trying to find a workable solution to this problem. Where it seemed appropriate we used both *he* and *she*. However, we feel it is our responsibility to make the book as easy to read and comprehend as possible. Where the use of both pronouns make reading the section more difficult, we have used the traditional he to mean both *he* and *she*.

I   Introduction

There are a number of reasons to consider buying a going business. If you are looking to get into business, buying an existing company is usually the quickest, most cost effective and least risky method of entry. If you own a going business looking to expand, an acquisition can be the most efficient way for you to gain new markets, new customers, and new capabilities.

Despite many of the advantages of buying a business, the acquisition process can be a difficult and often frustrating proposition. Many novices have unrealistic expectations regarding the ease of finding a business, the extent to which owners are willing to provide financing, and the appropriate methods of arriving at a reasonable price to offer for the business. The no-risk acquisition that will earn high income for its new owner on day one, unfortunately is tough to come by.

Buying a company is hard work. Finding an acceptable *target* is difficult in and of itself. From there, figuring out how you as the new owner could profitably operate the business takes considerable thought and planning. Then, you must analyze and verify reams of financial and other information. Finally, you must negotiate price and terms with an owner who very likely feels that you are buying not only his business but years of his sweat and toil, for which he expects to be compensated.

Despite the difficulties and obstacles, if you are realistic and persistent, you can be well rewarded for your efforts. Buying is often a better path than starting from scratch. Some of the advantages include:

- **Financing** — Banks tend to view acquisitions more favorably than they view startups. Bankers are trained to discount an entrepreneur's claims and dreams, and to rely instead on financial statements that demonstrate past performance. The startup has no such past performance, making the banker's job of analyzing financial statements quite impossible. However, the buyer of a going business will have past financial statements making it possible for the banker to do what he or she is trained to do — analyze them. Having past financials available, provides a common prerequisite for gaining bank financing.

  Also, if you plan to buy rather than start a company, you may have the option of borrowing some part of the needed funds from the seller. While sellers don't like to *take back paper* any more than they have to, most buy/sell deals do involve some amount of owner financing. In our experience, owners will typically finance 20% to 50% of the deal.

- **Established Customer Base** — It is often said that a business starts with a customer. A going business, at least one that deserves serious consideration, will have an existing base of customers. A startup company will not, except in certain unusual circumstances, have customers at the onset. When you buy a business, this customer base is much of what you are buying.

- **Less Set-up Time** — Starting a company takes a tremendous amount of time. Typically, a startup entrepreneur must buy equipment and supplies, set up an appropriate space, get phone and electricity installed, etc., etc. A going business has done this already, so much time can be saved.

- **Lower Risk** — Any small business venture is risky. However, a going business with a good history is generally less risky than a startup. A going business has at least been able to survive for a period of time. The concept has been tested in the marketplace, and presumably the ways of doing business have been honed and modified along the way. Consequently what you are buying are the benefits of a good deal of trial and error learning.

By purchasing a business, you are purchasing a great shortcut into the world of small business. Buying a going firm can also be a great opportunity for an existing business to expand more quickly than through any of the more traditional means of growth. Unfortunately, the buy/sell process is often not understood by would-be buyers, sellers, and even by intermediaries such as lawyers, accountants, and business brokers. Because so few people have ever bought or sold a company, finding experienced advisors can be as difficult as it is important.

This book will take you through the key steps of the buy/sell process and explain each step. It will also point out some of the more common mistakes and pitfalls inherent in the process. In writing it we have tried to be as succinct as possible. We have also tried not to over-glamorize the process or mislead the reader into believing it is easier to find and buy a business than it really is. At the same time, we have tried to point out the very significant opportunities that can be exploited through business acquisition. Most importantly, we have tried to write a no-nonsense guide to the steps necessary for a successful business acquisition.

Finally, note that much of this book is written for individuals or groups purchasing going companies. For companies buying other companies, the goals are sometimes quite different. We have included a special chapter that directly addresses *growth through acquisition*, or companies buying other companies (Chapter IX).

What Kind of Business?

Often, the first question that comes to mind when one is thinking about purchasing (or starting) a business is: "What kind of business do I want?" and "How will I be functioning within that business?" "What will I be doing as the owner of the business?"

The first question you may ask is, "What kind of business should I buy?" While some of us have a definite idea about the kind of business we want, others do not. In either case, it is important that you know how you will be spending the majority of your working time. It is easy to misjudge the functions of the business owner. The owner of a restaurant, for example, doesn't necessarily cook.

We know a man who spent many years working for a computer company where he was involved in programming as well as teaching. When an opportunity came along to buy a franchise to open a school for computer programming, he felt it was the ideal opportunity. Six months after opening the school he realized that business management was not for him, and he sold out to his investing partner.

What he learned was that the owner of a computer programming school doesn't always get involved with teaching or programming or computers — people are hired to do those things. The owner must manage the business. While managing in a large company means planning and supervising, in a small company it means that and often more. The owner/manager of a small company like this computer programming school must also worry about a broken projector, a janitor who fails to clean a classroom, collecting overdue tuition, and many other distasteful duties. There is no one to pass final responsibility on to, no matter how grand or small the responsibility might be.

Helen M., who is a graduate of the Rhode Island School of Design, always wanted to buy a store where she could utilize her clothing design skills. When a bridal shop that had been in existence for about forty years came on the market, she bought it. She immediately began to devote a substantial amount of her time to altering and customizing gowns and to introducing her own designs.

After about a year and a substantial dip in volume, she realized that she should have been devoting her energies to selling what the manufacturers were offering in the current season rather than to attempting to design new styles, or to modifying clothes for customers' special needs. That is the way the shop had been successful in the past — catering to the needs and wants of the customers, not the needs and wants of the owner.

The message here is that it is very important to know what it is that the owner of a business does on a day to day basis. If you are planning to enter an industry that is different from your employment experience, it may be to your advantage to get a job in that field just to get a feel for what an owner does, before you actually have to do it .

Find a Niche, Find a Niche!

Once you have decided on a field of business, you still have to decide what kind of business within the field is your best opportunity. Often the most satisfying, most profitable, and most enduring businesses are those that have a unique aspect or a *niche* in the marketplace. This uniqueness or niche may be the result of a variety of factors. Sometimes it results from size. We know of a mail order business with a steady, repeat clientele. It takes very little effort to run, grosses about $35,000, and nets about $25,000 per year. The unique quality is its size: It's too small to entice much competition, as is its market as a whole.

Another example of a perfect niche: Harold B. owns a Grade B downtown hotel, which he bought a couple of years ago. A small, Grade B hotel that is well managed and efficient can be profitable, and in many cities, it is essentially immune from competition. Today's building economics are such that nobody can profitably build a Grade B hotel downtown. People build Grade A hotels which, after thirty years, may become Grade A-, and, after thirty more years will become Grade B. In short, his little B hotel niche is secure for quite some time to come.

We know of another businessman named Jerome who has found a comfortable niche. He owns a business that sells and services microscopes. He represents a couple of manufacturers, but in the microscope business, the profits from equipment sales are small because the competition is quite stiff. The bulk of his profit comes from trade-ins and from service. Laboratories, research institutes, and universities that are *locked-in* on the use of a particular brand of microscope tend to come back to the same company for service, trade-ins, and other needs, thus becoming a captive market.

Finding that niche in the marketplace, whether it is due to geography, economics, an unusual set of circumstances, or a unique service or product-line, can make all the difference. Most smaller businesses that do well owe their success in part to serving a well-defined niche.

II Why Sellers Sell

If you think like many buyers do, the first question you may ask about a potential business for sale is, "Why is the owner selling?" While we don't discount the need to ask the question, we do feel it is given too much importance in the minds of prospective buyers.

It is not unusual to enter a potential buy/sell situation with a great deal of healthy suspicion. The predominant suspicion seems to be, "This guy knows his business is in big trouble, and that's the reason he wants to sell it to me. After all, if the business had a good future, why would he want to sell it?"

The fact is that there are a myriad of reasons why a seller might want to sell. We won't deny for a second that one of those reasons can be that the business may be heading for a problematic or even a disastrous future. Later we'll present a number of evaluative techniques to help you assess the future of a business, regardless of the owner's motivation for selling.

Probably the most trusted reason for selling, from a buyer's perspective, is retirement. If a seller says that he is selling because he wants to retire (providing he is of retirement age), most buyers' suspicions are alleviated. Shrewd sellers, of course, know this, so if they are in their late fifties or older, they may indicate that this is one of the reasons for selling whether or not it is true.

Divorce settlements and health problems closely follow retirement as *acceptable reasons* for selling one's company.

What you may not so easily accept is that there are other reasons for selling that are completely legitimate. If you were buying a car or a house would you be very concerned with an owner's reason for selling? Even if you were buying stocks and you knew that the seller may well be selling because he assumes the stock is on the way down, would you change your mind about buying that stock? Or would you instead decide to proceed based on your own different judgments or different investment needs than those of the seller?

Before getting into reasons for selling, we think it's appropriate to discuss some common misunderstandings about small businesses, and especially about the people who own them. It is these misunderstandings that lead prospective buyers to the erroneous assumption that owners don't sell decent businesses unless they are retiring.

The Myth of the Entrepreneur

In recent years the image of the entrepreneur has risen from that of an unscrupulous opportunist to nearly that of a folk hero. No longer are entrepreneurs perceived as con artists who will do just about anything to make a buck. Now they are perceived as innovators, builders, and doers who can overcome all obstacles to attain their companies' goals. Those companies now, by popular image, are not sweat shops or amoral entities that exist only to make a profit for their owners. They are instead entities that will help us all transcend the problems of the past and enter a brave new world.

The popular image of today's entrepreneur is that of a well educated young person tossing aside a hundred career options to pursue a new venture — a new vision. He or she is tireless, arriving at the office by 6 am and returning home late at night if at all. During that time this mythical entrepreneur maintains a high level of energy as he or she wows bankers, investors, customers, and, of course, motivates employees to peak performance. This storybook entrepreneur is fearless in his pursuit to succeed and will overcome whatever obstacle may be in his path.

In reality few entrepreneurs can meet this romantic profile. What's more, most every field has its *overachievers*. While some entrepreneurs may approach the mythical profile, we're not convinced that small business has any more of a claim to superstars than does law, medicine, sports, or education.

The vast majority of small business owners are normal people that face the same sets of needs, problems, and life changes as do the rest of us.

The Myth of the Small Business

Those who don't own businesses and even some of those who do tend to have a romanticized view of business ownership.

It is a common misconception that just about any small business that has survived for a few years is almost automatically making lots of money. In reality, the vast majority of small companies are not providing huge incomes for their owners. Undoubtedly some are; but most are not. We believe that many small business owners could probably earn more money by working for someone else than in running their businesses. This is especially true if income is calculated on an hourly basis — so many business owners work long hours which, of course, dilutes their earnings per hour.

Further, the day to day work of most entrepreneurs is neither glamorous nor romantic. A typical day is spent putting out brush fires, dealing with various problems, and getting the work out the door.

Our point is this. There are small business owners out there who would consider selling their companies. The fact that they would sell does not necessarily indicate that the owner thinks the business is doomed.

Reasons for Selling a Company

The owners of some very well run and profitable companies may, under the right set of circumstances, be willing to sell. It depends on, among other things, their needs and life situations at the time, the offer itself, and the options that the seller perceives for himself or herself. An entrepreneur may consider leaving a good business for the same kinds of reasons that an employee may consider leaving a good job.

Some of the legitimate reasons why sellers sell are as follows:

- **Retirement**

  As stated above, retirement is the most acceptable reason for selling a business, in the view of many buyers. While this is a fine reason for selling, don't make the mistake of totally believing a seller who claims retirement plans. Firstly, retirement can so easily be the stated reason without being the actual reason. Oftentimes once a seller who is at or near retirement age states this as a reason for selling, prospective buyers drop their guard and become less suspicious than perhaps they should be. That is, retirement is often the stated reason while it is not the actual reason.

  Secondly, a retiring owner typically feels little pressure to come to a buy/sell deal. An owner who plans the sale of his or her business in advance can decide, "When I'm about 60, I'll start looking at the idea of selling. If it takes three months to find a buyer at my price, that's fine. If it takes three years, that's fine too." A seller in this situation would not be a likely candidate for selling at a bargain price, whereas an owner who is anxious to make a deal quickly might well be willing to listen to a less generous offer.

- **Owner is Bored or Fed up with the Business**

  Despite the entrepreneurial myths, many small business owners simply get bored with their businesses. Buyers tend to be especially suspicious of this as a reason for selling. After all, small business is played up to be the greatest most exciting pursuit there can ever be. How is it possible for an owner of a successful business to get bored and give it up? The fact is it happens. Some people get more of a thrill from starting a business than from running it after the startup phase. Others go into it with misconceptions of what small business ownership entails on a day to day basis. The bottom line is boredom and frustration can occur in small business ownership just as it can in any other career direction.
  A seller recently told us, "I want to sell my company because I've been at it for 8 years, and I'm just bored with it. I'm no longer devoting the energy to it that I should be. If my business were failing, I'd have no choice but to get out. If I were getting rich from it, I would probably be more willing to put up with the boredom. The fact is I'm making a living from it, and that's all. Someone can come in here with the energy and enthusiasm that I had when I started the company and grow this business quickly. But I've had it, and I want out."

  This is not an uncommon sentiment among small business owners despite the lore of the entrepreneur. There are businesses out there with jaded owners who don't have the drive or the energy to exploit their company's potential. This kind of company can be a great opportunity for a buyer with the energy and drive to *make it happen.*

- **The Need for a Regular Paycheck**

Business ownership is a risk. An established business that is thriving will generally pay its owners a regular salary on a weekly or monthly basis. Any money left over after the salaries and expenses are paid (profits) will either be reinvested into the company or paid out to the owners, over and above salary.

However, many less than rock solid small companies can not pay their owners' salaries on a regular basis, let alone earn profits. Some just don't have the money available so they can't pay it. Others may pay their owners adequately but irregularly. While the former situation is probably not a great business opportunity (except possibly for a company to company acquisition), the latter may be.

For example, it may be that the owner who is getting paid irregularly needs more stability due to a life change or a psychological change that demands income stability. For a buyer who can live on a few big paychecks rather than a lot of smaller ones, this kind of situation may offer a reasonable opportunity.

- **A Good Offer Comes up**

Those of us who make part of our living buying and selling businesses, sometimes bluntly ask business owners the unsolicited question, "Do you want to sell your company?" A typical response is a long pause followed by a statement of, "Yeah if the price is right." Small business ownership represents a lot of different things to different people. One thing it represents in nearly all cases is an investment. Many owners reason that if they can earn a good profit by selling that investment, they'll sell it.

Clearly, this can be a win-win situation. It is well within the realm of reason to expect that you can get a good deal from your perspective, while a seller can earn a profit from the transaction. If this were not the case, our free market system couldn't operate because goods and services couldn't change hands to the mutual advantage of buyers and sellers.

- **Family Life Changes**

Any number of family changes can lead to a decision to sell a company. The birth of a child, an older child going off to college, a divorce, or a death can all lead to a business for sale.

While it is not unwise to be suspicious of family changes as reasons for sale, if those changes are believable, they may well be legitimate. Sometimes family changes can put pressure on a seller to sell quickly which can mean a better negotiating position for you.

- **Spouse Job Change**

It is very common for a husband to get an out of town job offer and for his wife to sell her business as a result. It is less common but by no means unheard of for a wife to change jobs and her husband to sell his company as a result. In either case this is a perfectly legitimate and understandable reason for an owner to want to sell.

This situation may mean the seller will be in a hurry to sell and may be willing to consider a lower price. In some unusual cases, part of the job offer may include a stipulation that the employer may compensate the employee (and spouse) for financial loss if the business has to be sold for a lower price than it is worth. In this case, the seller may be even more willing to listen to your low offer, resulting in a bargain opportunity for you. Again, guaranteeing the price of a business by an employer is rare but not unheard of.

- **Business Owner Gets Job Offer**

Conventional wisdom states that no self-respecting entrepreneur would consider working for someone else except under the most dire circumstances. In reality, some entrepreneurs are fence sitters and could be happy either in their own businesses or working for someone else.

Recently the owner of a thriving retail store asked us to sell his business. Why? He had an opportunity to take a position as a newspaper reporter, his profession prior to entrepreneurship to which he wanted to return. He needed to let the paper know within two weeks so he was willing to sell for a rock bottom price. Obviously this was a great opportunity for a buyer interested in a retail shop.

- **Future Growth Limited by Management Abilities**

We are currently working with the owner of a thriving small company. He started his company about five years ago. Today he is earning about $135,000 per year and has little difficulty attracting business. His only problem is that he does not feel capable of running the business if it gets any bigger than it is.

He is a very competent machine builder by training. He does not like dealing with marketing, salesmanship, and especially with financial management. His ideal scenario is for someone to buy a controlling interest in his company (about 75%) and keep him on as an employee and part owner. One stipulation — the buyer would have to be a proven manager who could grow the firm into a mature and much larger company.

This kind of situation can be an unusually good opportunity for the right kind of buyer. There are other entrepreneurs out there who by luck or design found a marketplace need and filled it, but who are not skilled managers prepared to take the company into a phase of controlled growth. If you are that kind of skilled manager and can find this type of situation, you should jump on it without delay.

- **Need for Investment Capital**

There are young companies with bright prospects but without the dollars available to realize that potential. While the traditional solution is to seek venture capital (investors) some owners choose instead to sell the company to someone who can both run it and finance its growth. Typically the seller would remain as an employee and minority owner of the company. In essence this is similar to a venture capital deal except that the buyer takes a controlling interest (venture capitalists rarely do this), and the buyer runs the company (again, rare for a venture capitalist).

Chapter Summary

Surely, there are small business owners who try to *unload* problematic businesses on unsuspecting buyers. Buyers are usually most comfortable when the stated reason for selling is that the owner is retiring. The fact is that there are a host of legitimate reasons for a business owner to want to sell; retirement is only one of them. In fact, since shrewd sellers know that buyers like to hear that retirement is the reason for selling, this is sometimes the stated reason even when it is not the actual reason.

If you plan to buy a company, a certain amount of suspicion is well warranted. However, you should spend less effort on deciphering the reason for selling and more on verifying and researching the business — its past and current performance, its prospects, and the seller's claims.

III. Seller Perspective Versus Buyer Perspective

In the case of small privately held companies, sellers and buyers approach a buy/sell situation from very different perspectives. Understanding the difference may help you in talking to prospective sellers and may help you understand statements and attitudes that could otherwise cause grief, misunderstanding, and anger.

Emotional Attachment

To a seller, the sale of a business that he started and devoted much of his life to is a difficult proposition. We've worked with sellers who would almost have less difficulty divorcing their spouses or putting their children up for adoption.

Try to be sensitive to this emotional attachment. Don't make the mistake of treating the seller as if he were selling a used car that he just picked up last month. While to you, each business may be one more situation to check out, to a business owner, his business deserves more consideration and understanding than that.

An understanding of the emotional attachment is helpful. Few buy/sell deals go through when the buyer and seller feel animosity toward one another. Cooperation and mutual understanding pave the way for a deal far better than do perceived insults and disrespect. You must understand and be sensitive to the fact that a considerable amount of seller ego is tied up in the business.

Mutual Suspicion

If you are considering the purchase of a business, you are well justified in being suspicious of claims, inferences, and anything that just doesn't seem quite right. Your suspicions may include, "What is the seller trying to put over on me? What is he hiding? Does he want to sell because of a potential calamity that I don't know about?"

You should also realize that a seller approaches a buyer with apprehension as well. Typical fears are, "What if this guy wants to pump me for information so he can compete with me? What if he doesn't have any money? What if he takes this business that took me 20 years to build and runs it into the ground?"

There is no easy solution to this mutual suspicion as it is quite justified, at least initially. In many cases it often disappears or is at least lessened after buyer and seller get to know each other. If not, the likelihood of a deal is slim. Buying a business is not like buying a house or a car. After the transaction is completed, the buyer and seller do not just walk away from one another. They usually have to work together for at least a short time and sometimes for an indefinite period of time. For this reason the chemistry must be reasonably good. If it doesn't start off that way, it is unwise to expect improvement later in the relationship.

A good broker, or another intermediary, can sometimes be of help here. Sophisticated buyers and sellers will have their intermediaries "talk tough" and state objections. They reason, "Hey, if this deal goes through, we're going to have to work with each other. Let's not get into arguments and set the stage for a strained relationship." The intermediaries walk away afterwards and don't really have to worry about lingering bad feelings, arguments, intransigent positions, objections, or suspicions.

Past Reality Versus Future Potential

Entrepreneurs are noted for their optimism. Sellers are fond of telling buyers what they themselves are convinced of: "The future of this business is so bright that an analysis of past performance can't do it justice." It is a rare seller indeed who tells us that he expects next year to be less profitable than the current year.

You as the buyer may want to talk more about the past performance as it is shown in black and white via financial statements. While you may be equally as optimistic about the company's future, you should insist on valuing and buying the business based on past performance. If you do buy the firm, future improvements will be based on your efforts, not on those of the seller. Again, there is no easy remedy to this difference of perspectives.

Some Sellers Think that No One Else Can Run this Business

It is a common attitude among business owners that no one can run their companies as well as they can. It is also common for prospective buyers to look at a business and decide that they can easily do better.

A seller typically will assume that you will need months of training in the business before you can competently run it. You, on the other hand, may look at the business and figure anyone with half a brain can learn this business in a week. Obviously, communicating this to a seller who thinks his business is very complicated would be highly insulting.

Conversely, you should avoid the common temptation of thinking that you can buy a business and quickly increase sales and profits. Don't do as some novice buyers do and casually look over the operation and decide this employee can go, and this product can be sold to that market, etc. Seldom is improving a newly acquired business as quick and easy it seems.

In taking over a going business, you should change little if anything for the first few months of operation. Get a feel for the how and the why of the operation and its management practices. Once you understand the way things are, then gradually implement improvements that seem warranted.

IV What You Can Buy

While the question may seem simplistic, it is important to ask yourself, "What am I buying?" After all, you're shelling out thousands of dollars in the hope of obtaining benefits that justify the price. Exactly what are those benefits? Are they worth it?

A company is worth considering for purchase if you are convinced that you will receive adequate benefit for that purchase. That is, the acquisition should offer a more efficient route to a particular business goal than other available alternatives.

For example, Joe Smith may decide that he wants to be in the printing business. He wants the independence and the chance of higher income. While Joe is an experienced printer, he does not want to face the difficulty and risk of starting his own company. Further, he feels that his town can not support another print shop. Therefore, he reasons that buying one of the existing shops in town is his best strategy. He is buying his ticket out of the work and risk of startup, and into a place in a slightly less competitive market (one that does not include the new shop that he would otherwise have to start). Of course he is also buying independence and a chance for higher income, but starting his own shop would give him this as well.

In advising prospective buyers, we'll generally ask right up front, "What are you buying? You're spending all this money to buy a business. What value are you getting? Can you get better value for your money by starting your own business?" Surprisingly, only a little better than half of our clients can initially answer these questions.

While there are a number of reasons for buying a going business rather than starting a business, not all going businesses support all the reasons. Several of the concrete reasons for buying businesses (the tangible benefits that can be bought) are discussed in this section. If you're planning to purchase a company, make sure that you know its value to you.

Note that this section applies to both individuals and to existing companies that may be planning an acquisition. Chapter IX (Companies Buying Companies) applies specifically and exclusively to companies that wish to acquire other companies.

Low Risk

One of the chief reasons for buying rather than starting a business is to keep your risk as low as possible. Starting a business is inherently more risky than purchasing a going concern. In the case of an existing business looking to expand, purchasing a going business is a less risky method of getting new business, entering new markets, or adding production capabilities, than any of the more traditional methods.

Most of the other reasons for buying businesses are at least partly based on perceived lower risk. It's fair to say that the lower the perceived risk, the higher the value of the business. However, don't make the mistake of assuming that any business you buy will truly offer lower risk. You must clearly evaluate exactly how your risk will be lowered. Some of the lower risks of buying a business as compared to starting one come about because of:

- **Existing Customers** — No business can exist without customers. Seldom does a startup business have customers on the day it starts. A going business does have customers, and this is one of the main things it has to offer a prospective buyer. Even though those customers are probably free to go elsewhere, a well-executed acquisition should result in a high customer retention rate. The benefits of buying a customer base are discussed in more detail below.

- **Well-Developed Procedures and Practices** — Even an experienced entrepreneur faces a significant learning curve in entering a new business. It takes time to find out the best sources of supplies, inventory, and necessary business services.

- **Customer Needs** — Even more important and more difficult is learning how to please your customers. What do they want? How can the business best deliver what they want?

- **Learning Curve** — The learning process is inherently fraught with risk. It takes time to learn how best to run a business, and as a business owner time will be your key resource. Further, this kind of learning is often done by trial and error. Unfortunately, too many errors can literally mean the end of your business.

  A going business has probably gone through a long and arduous learning curve. As the new owner, the benefits of having done so can be passed along directly to you. This takes the form of in-place supplier relationships, procedures for dealing successfully with customers, advertising strategies that have (probably through trial and error) been effective, and a number of other management procedures that will shorten the learning curve, and thereby lower your risk.

- **In-Place Employees** — Unless you are planning to buy a business that you can operate by yourself, you will have to contend with personnel issues. You must retain competent labor and management in order to make the business work. A going business will have a staff in place, while a startup will not. Clearly, there is less risk in relying on a trained and experienced staff that knows how to work together than in relying on a new staff.

- **Lower Financial Risk** — As discussed elsewhere in this book (Chapter XI Financing a Deal), a key advantage to buying versus starting a business lies in financing. Banks and other traditional financing sources are less than thrilled about the prospect of lending to a startup company. In fact, they will seldom make startup loans unless the loan can be supported through a personal guarantee backed by collateral, usually real estate or stocks and bonds.

  However, in an acquisition, the seller typically supplies some of the financing through payment over time. More often than not, if the purchased business fails, all the seller gets is his business back, without recourse to other assets held by the buyer. Obviously this means that the buyer has a much lower downside risk if the worst happens and the business goes under.

Turnkey Business

Like most buyers, you are probably looking for a *turnkey* business or a business that can be easily taken over and run without a lot of training or a lot of modification. A business that you can walk right into and run profitably starting from day one should be worth more to you than one that will take time and effort to get up and running. Of course your own particular skills partly define the kind of business situations that you can easily take over.

If you can find a business that you can easily take over and run without a lot of training and practice, that business will be a less risky venture for you. We advise sellers to get the business operations out of their owner heads and into systems and operating procedures that a buyer can easily comprehend. Recently, we were involved in the sale of a business where the owner spent a year modifying the business so that it could be easily managed by a new owner with minimum initiation. He broke the business down into concise and easily understandable components. He then assigned each of his two employees to a number of components. To test the new structure, he stayed away from the office for one day, then two, then three, and so on. By the time he was ready to sell, he could honestly insure the new owner that the business could practically run itself.

Smooth Transition

Avoid companies that promise a rough transition period. In fact it is best to make as few changes as possible for the first few months after the ownership transition, and then to start gradually modifying the business as necessary. The degree to which the transition will be a smooth one, is an important criteria by which to evaluate a prospective acquisition. In most transitions it is essential that the seller (or manager) agree to remain with the business for an adequate period of time after the sale to help the new owner survive that transition and keep the business in smooth operation.

Base of Repeat Customers

The most important element of any business is its customers without them, there is no business. Customers that are *locked in* are worth more than customers that may easily take their business elsewhere, or customers that are one time (non-repeat) customers. For example, an insurance agency's customer base would command a premium value. Once these customers choose an agency, they tend to stay with that agency for a long time. In fact, customers perceive changing agencies as being complex. While some changing does take place, it is the exception.

Contrast that example with a company that installs and repairs residential driveways. Customers of this kind of company need service only on an occasional and irregular basis. When it comes time to fix a driveway or put in a new one, a customer may not even remember who he called last time, let alone feel any loyalty. This kind of customer base is worth much less.

Also, several small customers are worth more than a few large ones. If a few small customers are lost, it won't have a serious effect on the business. However if even one or two large customers leave, the effect will be painfully felt. A buyer should think about the implications very carefully before acquiring a company that is largely dependent on a few customers.

Synergies with Existing Company

It is not uncommon for one company to buy another with the goal of expanding its sales with no increase or only a small increase in expenses. For example, we recently helped sell a company that recruits dental hygienists and finds them temporary employment in dentists' offices. The company was not profitable although sales were reasonably good.

We approached a company in the temporary employment field, not of hygienists, but of office personnel. We convinced the latter firm that they could profitably take over the hygienist personnel business despite the fact that it was not making money. They could do so by using their own existing offices, personnel, computers, and even their existing forms to run the hygienist business. That is, they could take on the accounts without taking on the overhead. The office temporary firm bought the company. When the dental hygienist company's volume was added to the buyer's volume, it meant the buyer had a 35% increase in sales, literally overnight. However, the buyer's overhead expense increased only 9%.

This kind of acquisition is discussed in detail in Chapter IX.

Production Capabilities and/or Competitive Advantages

Sometimes a firm, or in unusual circumstances an individual, will acquire a company to gain access to production capabilities, proprietary or patented processes, favorable locations, or favorable supply contracts. For example, we know of a company that manufactures computer peripherals that bought a small software company, primarily to gain access to the seller's proprietary software. Had this manufacturer not been able to buy the software company, he would have had to hire programmers to develop appropriate software at much higher cost.

In another situation, the owners of a successful sandwich shop chain gave us a list of neighborhoods and said they would be interested in purchasing a small luncheonette or restaurant in any of those neighborhoods. They were buying desirable locations and in-place equipment. They converted each location to their own name and menu. It was cheaper to do this than to rent a space and buy and install equipment.

Trade Name or Trade Mark

A trusted product or company name can be a valuable asset worth purchasing. If you wanted to go into the business of marketing audio cassette tape, for example, the name *Sony* or *3M* would certainly help sales. This would be true even if the exact same tape were offered under a different brand name. That is, the consumer faced with a choice of a name brand audio cassette and an unheard of brand audio cassette is far more likely to choose the brand name, all else being equal. The same is true of a retail store. A store with a known name will in all likelihood sell more than a similar store without a recognized and established name.

It is not unreasonable to pay for the rights to a name that you believe will enhance market-ability. However, sellers tend to have an inflated concept of the worth of the names of their businesses. Nevertheless, an established, recognized, and trusted name may be a worthwhile asset in and of itself or as part of a business sale package.

Elimination of Competitors

Last year, the owners of a convenience store asked us to find a buyer for their business. We didn't have to look far. Its only nearby competitors, half a block away, bought the business almost immediately. The new owner closed the door on the store it had just bought and put up a sign referring customers up the block. Within three months the new owner raised his prices by 10%-20%. The price increase stuck because customers could no longer shop the two competitors for the best prices. While this example is a bit extreme, it is not uncommon for a buyer to buy out a competitor merely to create a less competitive marketplace.

Leapfrogging Startup

One reason to buy an established business is to save the time, energy, and the inherent risk of a startup. If you wanted to own an auto repair shop, you could buy the required equipment, rent a space and modify it to your needs, print stationery, order a phone line, and gradually gain customers. Another option would be to find an existing shop already set up, and to purchase that company. Of course if that company were profitable, it would command a significant premium for goodwill. But even if it were not profitable, buying it would save you the time and energy of setting up from scratch.

If your main reason for buying a company is to avoid the efforts of start-up, look for a company that is relatively new (a bit beyond startup but not yet mature), or a company that is in trouble but can be turned around. If it is the latter situation, insist on a low purchase price.

Be warned that sellers use this logic to establish value more readily than do buyers. We often hear from sellers, "To start a company like this would cost double what I'm asking; I know because I did it." However, if we were buying a company in that position we would tactfully argue that the seller made a bad investment but that doesn't mean we have to do the same. If you are buying a business solely to leapfrog startup as described here, there should be many acquisition choices open to you. There are no lack of companies for sale because six or twelve months into operations, the owner decides that he does not want to be an entrepreneur.

Before buying a company primarily to jump past the startup phase, be sure that the startup was reasonably well implemented so that undoing mistakes won't be more difficult than starting from scratch. Also, don't overpay based on the seller's evaluation of the work that went into it. It is probably worth only the value of tangible assets plus a very small premium (see Chapter VII Valuing the Business).

Diamonds in the Rough

It is somewhere between a buyer's hope and a buyer's fantasy to find a business that can be bought cheaply, improved easily, and either run very profitably or resold very profitably shortly after purchase. This is commonly referred to as a *turnaround.*

The reality is that these situations are hard, though not impossible to find. There are businesses to buy that are doing poorly and in need of a turnaround. The difficulty lies in finding the failing or underperforming company that can be turned around without a time consuming and expensive effort that is hard to justify.

The purchase of any company that is not operating profitably is at best a risky proposition, if it is to be run on a free standing basis. If you are willing to take the risks and the time to find such a firm, the potential rewards are very real. Some of the characteristics to look for are:

- **Owner(s) Lost Interest** — As discussed in Chapter II (Myth of the Entrepreneur section), despite conventional wisdom some business owners simply lose interest in their companies. When this happens sooner or later the business starts showing signs of neglect. These signs are easier to spot than are other business problems.

  For example, did you ever walk into an office and feel as if you were walking back in time? Occasionally, we will visit a client at his office and feel as if we've returned to 1965. The design is ancient; the company stopped keeping up with technological advances before touch-tone phones and long before desk top computers became omnipresent. Even the graphics on the stationery and the attitudes of the staff convey a feeling of an earlier time. If the company is a manufacturing company, and the production equipment is equally outdated, the problem is even more serious.

  This kind of situation indicates that the owner stopped being concerned with growing that business. Technological and other changes are important to the extent that they increase productivity and communicate that the organization is concerned with modern methods of better serving its customers.

Such a situation may indicate an opportunity for someone with the motivation to modernize the company. Be careful that you are looking to modernize the company not merely for the sake of modernization. Only if those modifications lead to higher efficiency, higher productivity, or somehow to a better bottom line are those modifications worth the effort from a business perspective.

A local liquor store provides a good example of an owner who lost interest in the company and a turnaround entrepreneur who exploited an opportunity. The store is in an excellent location. There are plenty of prospective customers in the area, and the town fathers decided not to allow any new liquor stores to open in this part of the city. This store featured dusty bottles, perennial stock-outs, and a clerk (usually the owner) parked in front of an old television set right next to the cash register. If a customer wanted to buy something, the staff was willing to sell it, but there was no assistance beyond that.

Further evidence of lost interest came in the form of the stock itself. While this neighborhood's drinking preferences have tended away from hard liquor and toward wine and other softer beverages, this store's product mix has remained the same.

About two years ago an entrepreneur asked the owner if he would consider selling. A deal was struck, one that made both parties very happy. The new owner cleaned up the store and dumped the old TV. He also changed the product mix to emphasize wine, beer, wine coolers and other products that were becoming more popular in the neighborhood. Further, he learned a lot about wine. He is always ready with an informed recommendation if called upon to provide one. The staff that did no more than ring up sales was replaced with one that helps customers to the extent necessary, including carrying boxes to their cars.

The new owner was smart enough to realize that he was gaining access to a great market where access was restricted by the town fathers. He understood that the store was a potential gold mine that was not being realized, only because the owners were not motivated enough to do the work necessary to realize that potential.

Spotting and exploiting a situation like this one has made many an entrepreneur rich in a relatively short period of time.

- **Clear Problem(s) that are Solvable** — To find a business with problems to solve is not enough to qualify an opportunity as a diamond in the rough. That opportunity must feature a clear problem(s) that the buyer can solve without serious difficulty.

For example, we are often told by would-be sellers that their struggling businesses could really do well with the right marketing. So, they reason, "We just need a buyer who knows how to market." The fact is, just about any business can do well with the right marketing. It's a matter of knowing what that right marketing is and having the resources to implement an appropriate marketing plan.

A diamond in the rough opportunity would be one where the prospective buyer not only recognizes the key problem, but also understands how to implement a solution. For example, we just helped a buyer with the purchase of a software firm. The selling company was founded by an engineer who developed a manufacturing control software package. The buyer, who has a strong background in manufacturing control, was impressed with the software's capabilities. He agreed with the seller that the problem was in marketing. However, the buyer was familiar with marketing practices in the industry and with a lot of the people in the industry that could make software buying decisions. He devised a marketing plan that relied on trade shows and on video presentations. He bought the company at a great price and was able to sell the software quite successfully based on his contacts and his industry knowledge.

Sometimes a company's key problem lies in financing. Here again, many a seller claims that with capital the business would enter the stratosphere. That's not enough. This situation qualifies as a diamond in the rough opportunity only if you understand exactly how new capital could be used, and the results that it would attain.

We are currently working on a situation where money is a big part of the selling firm's problem. The company is doing well in designing and building industrial production equipment. However, it is literally turning down work from major companies because those companies will not pay one-third in advance, and the owner does not have ready access to financing. If he did, volume and profits could nearly double overnight. To a buyer with adequate funds or adequate access to funds, this can be a tremendous opportunity.

Diamond in the rough or turnaround opportunities are out there. But they are not really opportunities unless the buyer knows what needs doing and has the skills and resources to do it. What may be a turnaround opportunity to a buyer with the specific skills necessary to the situation, may be a path to disaster for someone else.

Unfortunately, every seller of a failing company believes that the company can be turned around, while few have a good handle on how the turnaround can be achieved. Saying this business has great potential with "the right marketing" or with "more capital" is unacceptably vague from the perspective of a buyer. The buyer must be the final judge of the potential and of his or her ability to realize that potential.

V   Finding a Business to Buy

There are a number of ways that you can search for a business to purchase. Don't expect your search to go quickly; it is a difficult and lengthy process. This section outlines some of the ways that we have found to be effective methods to search for a company. Even in the best of circumstances, finding a business to buy is a hit and miss proposition. Therefore, we feel that it is best to use several of these methods concurrently until you achieve your goal.

One thing that will save you a good deal of time in your search is a clear written summary of your criteria for a company to consider. This should include:

- **Size of Company** — Consider the size range for the kind of firm that you can afford, and the size that you feel comfortable owning and running.

- **Industry** — We find that people who say they will consider a company in any industry seldom buy a business. Decide in advance on the kinds of industries that you will consider. You don't need to be overly specific, but at the very least decide the areas that you do not want to consider.

- **Geography**— What areas will you consider? Commuting distance may seem like a minor consideration in the scheme of things, but it is not so minor when you have to face a long and unwelcome commute each day. Of course if the company can be easily moved, that lessens the importance of location.

- **Profitability** — Are you looking for a company that is currently profitable (and are you willing to pay the price for it)? Or, is a turnaround based on your own expertise something to consider? While the advantages to buying a profitable firm are clear, turnaround businesses are easier to find and cheaper to buy.

These are some of the items to consider in advance. Of course different buyers have different needs. You may have a specific list of criteria that must be met. Think about it, and write it down. Doing so may take an hour or two now, but it will save you many more hours of unproductive looking later.

Some of the methods to use and places to look for possible opportunities are:

- **Local Newspaper**

  Probably the most common place to start a search for a business to buy is the local newspaper. The classified section will generally contain a listing of businesses for sale. Most papers use the heading Business Opportunity to designate the appropriate section. Sunday is almost always the best day to look; it will have the most listings. While local papers are the most common place to look, they are not always the best place to look. For smaller retail firms, service firms, and restaurants, it is a good place to start. For other kinds of businesses, there may be better search options.

- **Regional Papers**

  If you live in a smaller city, suburb, or rural area, the classified section of a nearby major metropolitan paper may be a good place to check. Even some companies in your own area may bypass the local paper in favor of an ad in the nearby major metropolitan paper. This is especially true of larger firms, and firms that want to try to keep the fact that they are for sale confidential in the local area.

- *The New York Times*

  The New York Times lists businesses for sale. While the paper is ostensibly local to New York, another edition is circulated nationally. In the daily paper, business opportunity advertisers can advertise in the City edition (which includes New York City and its suburbs, and part of New Jersey and Connecticut), the national edition, or both. On Sunday, all business opportunity ads are run nationally. The Times business opportunity section is nicely classified by type of business. If you are looking for a business in the New York area, checking here is essential. Even if you are looking elsewhere, this paper is worth a look, especially on Sundays.

- *The Wall Street Journal*

  The *Journal* is one of the nation's premier business publications. The paper is published in several regional editions. Sellers can and often do advertise only in their own region. The *Journal* lists business opportunities in a section called *The Mart*. Business opportunities are featured on Thursdays (there is no paper on weekends or holidays). It is generally used by sellers of larger small businesses and medium size businesses.

- **Trade Journals**

  Most industries and professions are serviced by a variety of publications geared specifically to the concerns of that industry. A good number of these publications accept classified advertising. If you are concentrating your search on a particular field or fields, trade journals are worth a look. Along these same lines, it might be a good idea to contact the trade or professional associations in the fields that you are searching. They might have a publication that contains classified advertising, or they may have a similar vehicle for buying and selling businesses. At the very least, the association should know what the industry publications are, and where to find them.

  You can learn about associations servicing virtually every industry and profession in the *Encyclopedia of Associations* (see Appendix).

- **Wholesalers and Suppliers**

  Wholesalers, suppliers, and their sales representatives often have inside knowledge of the goings on in the industries which they supply. If, for example, you are interested in buying a print shop, the people that sell ink, paper, and machinery to printing companies might know of potential opportunities.

- **Business Brokers**

  You might come in contact with a broker by choice or by necessity. That is, if you answer an ad in the paper, and the business is being handled by a broker, it is by necessity. You might also call around to the various brokers in your area and explain what you are looking for. Some brokers will perform searches for a reasonable fee. Dealing with brokers is discussed in detail in Chapter VI.

- **Your Employer**

  It is not uncommon for an employee or a group of employees to purchase a business from their employer. The only warning here is that employers (and employees) tend to be uncomfortable with the new dynamics of the relationship after the subject has been broached. While many employees feel they are capable of running the business, this may be a threatening concept to the employer.

  However, some of the smoothest sales that we have seen are those to employees. As an employee, you may be familiar with the day to day operations of the company, as well as its strengths and weaknesses. You probably know several of the customers and the suppliers. Much of the healthy suspicion with which a buyer approaches a seller can be avoided if the buyer already knows the business.

- **Direct Mail**

  You can approach businesses in your chosen industry via direct mail. We recommend a first class letter simply stating that you are interested in purchasing a company in a specified industry. A sentence or two about your background and hints of financial capability could be helpful. You can obtain lists from list brokers or from direct mail list companies. For a list of mail list companies see Direct Mail Lists Rates and Data, published by Standard Rate and Data Service in the library, or the Manhattan Business to Business yellow pages. Some libraries also retain copies of direct mail company catalogs. Thanks to advances in computers, list technology has attained a level of sophistication so that you can target precisely by zip code, industry type, and in some cases by size.

  Another source of lists is *Dun and Bradstreet* (listed in most local telephone directories). D & B can provide detailed lists of companies in virtually any geographical area in the U.S. Its lists include the owner's name, address, phone, sales volume, number of employees, and more. While D & B lists are more detailed, they are also more expensive than most list firms charge.

  Even with highly targeted direct mail efforts for buying a business, a response rate of 1% or 2% is pretty good, if you are approaching businesses that have not indicated that they are for sale. That is the projected rate for responses, not necessarily for responses that are worthy of follow-up.

- **Telemarketing**

   This area of direct marketing is increasing in popularity. For finding businesses to buy, though, we have mixed feelings about it. Asking an owner if he wants to sell his company, is nearly akin to hitting him on the head with a baseball bat. It will certainly get his attention, but he might be too shaken up to respond appropriately. Unlike a direct mail letter, a telephone query gives little time to regain one's composure and consider a response. It is easier to just say the equivalent of "no way." Despite our own reservations, there are people who have successfully found businesses to buy with this method.

- **Accountants**

   Often when an owner is considering selling, he will first discuss it with the firm's accountant. Therefore accountants often know of opportunities before anyone else does. However, accountants won't violate client confidentiality. Unless a client has specifically authorized the accountant to let the word out, the accountant will be silent about it. Also, accountants do not consider the sale of a client's business to be good news. He is losing a client if the sale is consummated. Possibly assuring an accountant that if he brings you a seller and you buy the company, that you will keep him as the firm's accountant would help.

- **Lawyers**

   Lawyers often obtain advance knowledge of possible businesses for sale. In some instances, lawyers are actually engaged by the client firm to find buyers. It couldn't hurt to pass the word that you are looking, to any lawyers that you know.

- **Bankers**

   Like accountants and lawyers, bankers sometimes get advance knowledge of businesses for sale. Bankers are not known for being loose lipped, but it couldn't hurt to let banker friends know that you are looking.

- **Business Associates**

   As with business in general, some good contacts can be made through networking for possible acquisitions. Letting business people know that you are interested in buying and in your criteria for a purchase could only help.

- **Bankruptcy Court**

   If you are looking for a turnaround situation or if you want to buy a firm as a synergistic addition to an existing business, you may want to check here. Every bankruptcy filing is public information, as is the list of filings. We know of people who visit their local bankruptcy court office weekly to search for possible opportunities of businesses that can be bought for bargain prices. You can find the nearest bankruptcy court by checking the phone book, or by calling the local number for federal government information.

A bankruptcy judge has the option of appointing a trustee (usually a lawyer) to handle the sale of a bankrupt firm's assets. If the judge has appointed a trustee, you will need to negotiate with that trustee, not the bankrupt firm's owner. Even without a trustee, the owner needs approval from creditors before making a deal to sell what's left of the firm. Consult with your lawyer before getting involved with a bankrupt company.

Despite the difficulties, buyers have cut deals to take over bankrupt firms for pennies on the dollar.

VI Business Brokers

A business broker's job is to find buyers for businesses that are for sale, and to put buy/sell deals together. While this sounds easy, it is a difficult undertaking. The fact is, few of us have any direct experience in buying or selling a company. Someone who knows the intricacies of the process, who also is in touch with businesses that are for sale, can be an important asset to a prospective buyer.

However there are a number of problems in relying on brokers to find an appropriate business for you and to bring a deal to successful fruition. Some of the benefits and difficulties in using business brokers are outlined in this section, along with advice on how to best utilize the services of brokers.

Brokers Work for the Seller

In most instances a business broker has an agreement with the seller that spells out what that broker will do, and how he or she will be compensated for the services rendered. Typically, a broker receives a commission for the successful culmination of a sale during a specified time period, based on a percentage of the selling price. It is important to understand that the broker is contractually obligated to work for the seller, not the buyer. He or she is in a sense a commissioned sales representative for the seller. He or she gets paid only for satisfactorily performing a specified service for the seller, namely selling the business. Further, a business broker, as any broker paid on a commission basis, is motivated to get the highest price for the seller.

There is nothing wrong with this arrangement as long as you understand that the broker is not an impartial intermediary. It is his job to present the business in the best possible light on behalf of his employer, the seller. If you feel that you need independent advice, seek it from someone other than the broker of the transaction at hand. You might want to independently hire a business broker on a fee basis to evaluate a deal and generally assist with it.

Brokers are Listing Driven

Not only do brokers usually work for the seller based upon a contractual arrangement, but most brokers think in terms of selling the *inventory* that they have available. That is, brokers are listing driven, not buyer driven. They find a business for sale, obtain a listing agreement from the owner(s), and then set out to sell that company. Few brokers will spend a lot of time or money searching for a business for a prospective buyer to buy. From the broker's point of view, working for the seller makes sense; it is easier to sell what you have available than what you don't have available.

It is more difficult for brokers to find a quality business for sale, than it is to find a buyer for a quality business. Therefore, it makes more sense for a broker to expend time and effort finding good businesses, than it does to spend time and effort searching for buyers. Once a profitable company in an attractive industry is listed by the broker, finding the buyer can be as easy as checking through his or her list of serious prospects.

Brokers Don't Like Very Small Firms

Brokers are generally paid on a commission basis. Therefore it makes financial sense for them to sell larger businesses than smaller ones. Brokers shy away from representing very small companies because often it is not worth the time and effort to sell such a company.

Often, brokers will impose a minimum commission of $7,000 to $10,000 or more. This has the effect of eliminating very small businesses from listing with a broker. This, of course, means that on a $50,000 transaction, for example, a broker will take 20% of the sale price, if the minimum commission is $10,000. Many businesses owners consider that to be just plain too expensive. So if you are looking for a company that is too small by broker standards, brokers may not be very helpful to your search efforts.

Screening Buyers

A major element of a broker's job is screening buyers. The broker is trying to eliminate non-serious prospects so as not to waste his time and the time of his client — the seller. The fact is that a broker gets lots of calls from prospective buyers. A broker knows that most of those callers will never buy a business. Some are merely *tire kickers* who want to talk about buying businesses and even to look at firms for sale, but not buy them. Others would like to buy, but are unrealistic about financing. There are even some who want to spy — to check out the businesses for sale and learn as much as they can about them for ulterior purposes.

Because buyers of quality businesses are easier to find than are sellers of quality businesses, a broker would rather screen out a few good prospects, than waste time with a lot of non-buyers.

Finally, a lot of sellers use brokers in part to protect confidentiality. A broker as an intermediary is an added layer of protection against too many people finding out that a business is for sale. For this reason, brokers are appropriately guarded about revealing too much information and risking a prospect's figuring out who the seller is, before broker and seller are ready to release that information.

Passing the Broker's Screening Process

Knowing that a business broker is charged with the responsibility of screening prospective buyers, and knowing that most brokers would rather err on the side of screening too tightly, your first job is to get through the screen. You must convince the broker to take you seriously and to actively try to help you find an appropriate company to buy.

The first step is to understand the broker's position and motivation. Unlike most selling situations, the broker feels he must cater to the needs of the seller, not to you, the buyer. In a typical sales situation, the sales person's job is to sell as much of what he has for sale as he can. In selling businesses, though, each product (the business for sale) is unique. Each can be sold only once; the usual dynamics of a salesperson-buyer encounter do not apply. The broker has the power, in fact the responsibility, to decide who is and is not a good prospect for any given business, and to politely screen out the less than serious.

Because people are accustomed to a different set of salesperson-buyer dynamics, one based upon virtually an unlimited supply of goods to be sold, buyers often make the mistake of overestimating the leverage they have with a broker. Usually, when a willing buyer with the means to make a purchase is ready to make that purchase, he or she will have little difficulty finding a salesperson ready to sell that product. It is an unusual situation indeed in our society when a wiling and able buyer can't go elsewhere to buy the same product. But in buying a one of a kind item like a business, that is indeed the situation.

In selling a business, a broker typically has an exclusive right to represent a company for sale. Unlike a real estate brokering situation, there is no equivalent to a multiple listing service (MLS), so there is no alternative path to buying the same property.

Finally, business brokers know that theirs is not a business that thrives on repeat sales. Most brokers will not put a high premium on keeping you happy in the interest of retaining your future business. While there are some exceptions, most brokers reason that they will never do business again with a buyer who just bought a business, so keeping that buyer's goodwill is of secondary concern.

Understanding the broker's motivations as they pertain to buyers, puts you in a better position to approach and deal with that broker. Like it or not, a broker is looking for a reason to discount you as a *serious prospect*. Because that broker probably has an exclusive agreement on each business listed for sale, you can not threaten to go elsewhere, if you are interested in one of his client firms. You must get and keep that broker on your side, not against you. Some suggestions on how to convince a broker that you are serious are listed below:

- **Know what You Want to Buy**

  Business Brokers generally frown on prospects who don't know what they want to buy. Some brokers will ask you right up front, "What kind of business are you looking for?" If you give a vague response, or worse a response of, "I'm not really sure," or, "It doesn't' really matter," then you will be quickly screened out. Brokers reason that a prospect who does not know what he is looking for is not a buyer. Be prepared with a clear crisp response to the question, "What are you looking to buy?" This doesn't mean that you have to know exactly the kind of business down to the last detail. It is perfectly reasonable to know you want a non-food retail store within 40 miles of your home, grossing between $500,000 and $1,000,000 per year. It is not necessary to be so specific as to state you want a toy store grossing $400,000 in the downtown area. Be ready to explain the industry, location, approximate size, and any other clear criteria to describe the type of firm you want to acquire.

An effective tool for convincing a broker that you are serious, communicating your needs to the broker, and for focusing your own mind on what you want to buy, is a written *acquisition summary*. An acquisition summary is a brief document that spells out what you are (and what you are not) interested in considering. Acquisition summaries are described in greater detail in Chapter IX.

- **Indicate a Knowledge of the Kind of Business You Plan to Buy**

Once a prospect passes the *What do You Want to Buy Test*, brokers try to determine how realistic the prospect is. A prospect who says the equivalent of, "That seems like a great industry," or, "My brother's friend made a pile of money in that business," will not be considered a great prospect. However, someone who says, "I've worked in that industry for 10 years," or, "I've worked in a related industry," or, "I've researched that industry and believe that it has a good future and that my skills are right for that kind of business," will pass to the next screen.

- **Prove Financial Capability**

Probably the most common complaint business brokers have is that of non-serious buyers wasting their time. Brokers are especially on the lookout for people who don't have access to the money needed to buy a business. More experienced brokers will politely but firmly ask about your financial situation early in the interview. He or she may ask, "So, how much money do you have," but the implication will be quite clear.

Be ready to be queried about your financial credentials. Typically a broker will want to know how you intend to pay for a business whether it is through savings, loans based upon your assets as collateral, etc. More important, be ready to prove that you are telling the truth if you want a broker to take you seriously. If a timid or inexperienced broker neglects to bring up this issue, it is a good idea to volunteer the information; even if he's not asking, he's wondering. A broker who knows that you have the financing is far more apt to expend effort on your behalf.

Indicate a Realistic Understanding of Financing

Unless you can convince a broker that you are capable of self-financing a deal, be prepared for questions about how you intend to finance your purchase beyond your own resources. Some of the red flags that brokers look for to screen someone out based on his being unrealistic about financing possibilities include:

- Not understanding that banks usually expect collateral.
- An unwillingness to use your home as collateral, even if there is no other collateral available.
- Misconceptions about small business loans being easy to obtain.
- Vague plans to *find a backer or investor.*
- Bad credit history.
- Unsubstantiated assurances that money is *no problem.*
- Plans to pay for a business nearly 100% from cash flow.
- Plans to pay for a business by leveraging (borrowing against) the acquired company's assets.

In most instances the bottom line is that a bank will lend money only to someone with solid collateral to support the loan. Some banks imply differently, but collateral is almost always required. With a few exceptions, the U.S. Small Business Administration also requires collateral in its lending and loan guarantee programs. To pass this screening you must convince the broker that you have cash or solid collateral that you are willing to pledge, or access to money from family or other non-bank sources.

- **Pay Broker to Do a Search for You**

  We (like some other business brokers and consultants) offer a search service to buyers. For a very modest fee, we will contact a specific group of businesses on behalf of buyers. For example, if a buyer is looking to buy a telephone answering service within 50 miles of Worcester, MA. our staff will contact all companies meeting that criteria and ask if they would consider selling their companies. We generally don't make money directly on this service; all we charge is out of pocket expenses. However, we reason that a prospective buyer willing to spend even one or two hundred dollars on a search, is worth taking seriously. If the search successfully turns up an appropriate acquisition, everyone gets what he wants; the buyer gets the company, and we get our commission. Even if the search does not directly turn up the right acquisition, the buyer who paid to have the search done is noted as being a highly qualified buyer. When an appropriate business does become available, that buyer is one of the first prospects contacted.

- **Keep Calling**

  If we judge a prospect to be a *lukewarm* possibility, we'll invite that prospect to call again in a few weeks to see if anything new has come up. The fact is that new businesses for sale come up all the time. If they are sold to the first prospect on the broker's list, those further down the line may never get called. If you call a broker(s) every few weeks, you will indicate to him that you are motivated to buy a company. Further, if your timing is right, you may learn about a business for sale earlier than you otherwise would have, if you waited for the broker to call you.

Like it or not, brokers categorize and rate prospects based upon statistics, personal experience, and hearsay. This section outlines the ways in which brokers categorize and rate prospective buyers.

- **Businesses and Business Owners** — Those who own at least one business are considered good prospects. They tend to be realistic about what is involved in buying and running a business, obtaining financing, and making a deal. Individuals who have previously bought a business are considered even better prospects still. Individuals who have bought a number of businesses can expect red carpet treatment.

- **Individuals with Previous Business Ownership Experience** — If you have had previous business ownership experience, you will be taken seriously by most brokers. It is common for someone who owned a business to get frustrated with working for a boss and to try to get back into business again. Stress previous business ownership experience when talking to a broker.

- **Individuals whose Parents are or were in Business** — Some brokers know that children from households where one or both parents were self-employed are more likely to go into their own business. Further, parents who own businesses and approve of their children doing the same may provide financial support for a business purchase. If one of your parents owned a business, even if only briefly, it may be worth mentioning.

- **Individuals whose Career to Date has been as a Big Company Employee** — Brokers are a little wary of people with this profile whether they are lower level employees or mid-level managers. Right or wrong, brokers feel that corporate employees tend to have misconceptions about the realities and difficulties involved in small business and tend to be risk averse.

  However, employees of large corporations are buying small businesses in increasing numbers. If you can convince a broker that you understand the realities and risks of small business ownership, your career background will not be a serious problem. Also, if you can convince that broker that you have the cash available, that fact will take precedence over your lack of small business experience.

- **Individuals who have Worked for Small Companies** — If you worked for a small firm, then you have experience with the realities of small business. Brokers look upon this kind of experience more positively.

- **Individuals Looking for a No-risk Deal** — The fact is that there are precious few *no risk* situations in small business. The few there are, are not for sale. Brokers know that their chances of coming up with a deal to satisfy someone overly afraid of risk is all but impossible.

- **Individuals who "Just had a Fight with the Boss"** — Brokers joke about disgruntled employees who call looking for a business to buy because, "their boss is a jerk." Long term dissatisfaction with working for someone else is a common reason for people to graduate to entrepreneurship. However, temporary dissatisfaction with one's work situation hardly ever leads one to purchase a company. Brokers know this and will screen out people who they perceive to be in this situation.

VII Valuing a Business

Business valuation is a mix of art and science. The bottom line is, of course, that a business is worth what a seller will sell it for, and what a buyer will pay for it. However there are ways of estimating a fair value. Several of these methods are described in this chapter. There are variations of these methods, and there are other methods that apply to specific situations. It is not uncommon to value a business by a number of different methods and use an average (or more likely a weighted average that gives more weight to some methods than to others) of the various methods used.

Note that there are a number of reasons for valuing a business, other than buying or selling it. Businesses are valued for estate and tax purposes, divorce settlements, and for raising capital. In keeping with the purpose of this book, all valuation discussions here will be limited to valuing for buying and selling purposes.

Value Versus Price

There are two important factors to consider when evaluating a business; one is *price*, and the other is *value*. They are often thought of as interchangeable although they have different meanings. The price of a business is the amount that the buyer will pay the seller. The value of a business is the amount that the business is worth to the buyer. The value is a more objective calculation that is based largely on the financial figures and to some extent on the expectation of the business's future profits. It can be used as a guideline to help you (and the seller) to arrive at the actual price. On the other hand, the price is influenced by many things, such as:

- How eager is the seller?
- How much of the selling price will the seller finance?
- Will the financing be at below market rates?
- Economic forecast for the industry

It could also be influenced by other factors such as competition. That is, how many other people are trying to buy the same business? Even seemingly small factors, such as the amount of training the seller is willing to provide as part of the price, will impact upon the price of a business. There are other such things that eventually will define the final price that will be paid for the business.

The value of a business, on the other hand, is derived independently of most of the above considerations. It is based on the assumption that the buyer will either pay all cash or will provide his or her own financing. The value of the business is also derived more on a financially rational basis which implies that the business is bought primarily for the purpose of making a profit.

It is important to ascertain the value of a business for several reasons. First, the process of carefully analyzing and working out certain adjustments to the financial information as presented by the seller can help you to uncover certain issues which the seller may be hiding or may not be aware of. Secondly, if you plan to get outside financing, the bank or other lender will expect to see this kind of formal evaluation of the business. Finally, you can sometimes use an objective valuation as a tool to demonstrate to the seller that his expectation of price may be unrealistic.

Capitalized Earnings Approach

A common method of valuing a business is called the *Capitalization of Earnings* (or *Capitalized Earnings*) method. Capitalization refers to the return on investment that is expected by an investor. There are many variations of how this method is applied. However the basic logic is the same.

To demonstrate the logic of this approach, suppose you had $10,000 to invest. You might look at different stocks, bonds, or savings accounts. You would compare the potential return against the risk of each and make a judgment as to which is the best deal in your particular situation.

The same return on investment logic holds for buying a business. Capitalization methods (and other methods) for valuing a business are based upon the return on your investment (as the new owner).

To further demonstrate the capitalization method of valuation, pretend that you are considering the purchase of a mythical and highly oversimplified business. Pretend the business is simply a post office box to which people send money. The magic post office box has been collecting money at the rate of about $10,100 per year steadily for ten years with very little variation. It is likely to continue to collect money at this rate indefinitely. The only expense for this business is $100 per year rent charged by the post office for the box. So the business earns $10,000 per year ($10,100-$100). Because the box will continue to collect money indefinitely at the same rate, it retains its full value. You should be able to sell it at any time and get back your initial investment.

You would probably look at this "no risk" business earning $10,000 and compare it to other ways of investing your money to earn $10,000 per year. A near no risk investment like a savings account or government treasury bills might pay about 8% a year. At the 8% rate, for someone to earn the same $10,000 per year that the magic PO box earns, an investment of $125,000 (125,000 x 8%= $10,000) would be required. Therefore, the PO box's value is in the area of $125,000. It is an equivalent investment in terms of risk and return to the savings account or T-bill.

Now the real world of small business has no magic PO boxes and no "no risk" situations. Business owners take risks, have expenses, and business equipment can and usually does depreciate in value. The higher that you believe the risk to be, the higher the capitalization rate (percentage) that you should use to estimate value. Rates of 25% to 40% are common for small business capitalization calculations. That is, a return on your investment of 25% to 40% is appropriate in buying a small business.

Finally, it is important to point out that the return on investment should be in addition to a fair salary for yourself or for a manager who you will hire. If you plan to devote your own work time in order to realize a profit, you should be paid a fair value for that work. The return on your investment must be over and above your fair and reasonable salary for the time you will spend working in the company. If you plan to hire a manager to run the company, that manager's salary must be included as an expense of the business before profits are calculated. For example, if the magic PO box produces $30,000 per year but requires a manager with a fair market salary of $20,000, the income for valuation purposes is $10,000, not $30,000. The fair market value for salary is the important number to use, not the actual salary to the current owner.

Excess Earnings Method

The Excess Earnings method (also called the Capitalization of Excess Earnings or CEE method), is the best valuation method for a wide range of small businesses. The basis of the method is quite simple. It states that the value of a business is equal to the net worth plus goodwill.

$$\text{VALUE} = \text{NET WORTH} + \text{GOODWILL}$$

The goodwill, in turn, is equal to a multiplier (which will be explained below), times the annual excess earnings. Again, earnings in this context excludes a reasonable salary to the owner.

$$\text{GOODWILL} = \text{MULTIPLIER} \times \text{EXCESS EARNINGS}$$

In simple terms, this means the value of a business is equal to the net worth — the inventory, fixtures, accounts receivable, etc. — plus a certain number of years of profit. That number, or multiplier, is typically somewhere between 1 and 6. Later (in the sub-chapter: "The Earnings Multiplier") we will discuss how to arrive at an appropriate multiplier. For the time being let's assume the multiplier is 3 (an average number). This means a business with a multiplier of 3 is worth the net worth plus a three year sum of excess earnings.

So a business with $30,000 of tangible net worth, excess earnings of $20,000, and a multiplier of 3 would be worth:

$$\text{GOODWILL} = \text{MULTIPLIER} \times \text{EXCESS EARNINGS}$$

$$\text{VALUE} = \text{NET WORTH} + \text{GOODWILL}$$

$$\text{GOODWILL} = 3 \times \$20,000 = \$60,000$$

$$\text{VALUE} = \$30,000 + \$60,000 = \$90,000$$

In the real world, it is not quite so simple. The financial statements provided by the seller usually need some refiguring before computing an appropriate value for the company. To illustrate this, let's pretend that you are considering the purchase of two companies. Both companies are roughly the same size in terms of gross revenues and in terms of *unadjusted* earnings. However, they are actually very different in terms of their adjusted earnings and in their financial requirements.

The first company, **Nurses Care, Inc.**, is a temporary employment agency for nurses. It requires only a few desks, a couple of typewriters, some stationery, and a phone to operate. The other company, **Harbor Locksmiths, Inc.**, is, as the name implies, a locksmith business. It requires a very substantial amount of assets to operate, such as merchandise, receivables, and so on.

Let's first look at the balance sheet (Example 1) and the income statement, often referred to as the "P and L," (Example 2) for **Nurses Care, Inc.**, which appear on the following pages.

The left column represents the figures as stated by the seller (or by the company's accountant). The column on the right represents the adjustments that you as the buyer need to make to the financial figures in valuing the company.

As we see in Example 1, there are few adjustments to the balance sheet. The only adjustment that really must be made is the long-term liabilities and capital items that are all lumped into one item equal to $6,524. Normally, the form in which the previous owner has capitalized the company is not important to the buyer. That is, whether the seller has financed the company with debt, equity, or a combination of the two doesn't really affect the value analysis. Therefore, it is best to simplify and show these numbers as one total item called *Capital*, or *Net Worth*.

Now let's look at Example 2, which is the income statement for the year ending December 31, 1990. Again, the left column represents the figures provided by the seller. The column on the right was added by us, to show relevant adjustments. The arrows indicate those items that have been changed.

Nurse Care Inc. Statement — Example 1

NURSES CARE, INC.

Balance Sheet at December 31, 1990

Assets

		Adjusted
CURRENT ASSETS:		
Cash in Bank	$ 6,779	
Accounts Receivable	11,001	
Prepaid Expenses	1,552	
TOTAL CURRENT ASSETS	19,352	
FIXED ASSETS:		
Furniture and Fixtures	1,750	
TOTAL FIXED ASSETS	1,750	
TOTAL ASSETS	21,102	

Liabilities and Capital

CURRENT LIABILITIES:		
Accounts Payable	8,394	
Accrued Taxes and Expenses	6,184	
TOTAL CURRENT LIABILITIES	14,578	
LONG TERM LIABILITIES:		
Loan from Owner	4,000	} 6,524
CAPITAL:		
Capital Stock, 1000 Shares	1,000	
Retained Earnings	1,524	
TOTAL CAPITAL	2,524	
TOTAL LIABILITIES AND CAPITAL	21,102	

Nurses Care P&L — Example 2

NURSES CARE, INC.

Statement of Income and Related Earnings
For the year ending December 31, 1990

Assets

			Adjusted
REVENUES	448,115		
Less – EXPENSES:			
Salaries Nurses	270,997		
Salaries Offices	34,115		
Salaries Owner	18,500	→	30,000
Taxes	14,054		
Office Expenses	4,564		
Repair and Maintenance	1,577		
Rent	25,385		
Telephone	12,662		
Insurance	2,389		
Advertising	14,662		
Legal and Accounting	2,470		
Utilities	1,763		
Auto Expenses	13,447	→	8,447
Interest Expense	2,700	→	0
Depreciation Expense	2,000	→	0
TOTAL EXPENSES	421,285		423,085
NET INCOME FOR THE YEAR	26,830	→	25,030
EXCESS EARNINGS			25,030

As you can see, the previous owner paid herself a salary of $18,500. Your position as the buyer is that a $30,000 salary is more appropriate for the amount of effort that managing this kind of business requires.

On the other hand, the auto expense of $13,447 included the use of an automobile by the owner. You feel that about $5,000 of that amount is a perk to the owner/manager, and not essential to operating the business. Therefore, for purposes of analyzing the company's value, $5,000 is deducted from the expenses (added back to owner compensation) in the adjusted (right hand) column on Example 2.

Also, we adjusted the amount that the seller paid in interest expense. In fact, we took it out completely, and put zero in the adjusted column. This does not mean at all that we are disregarding interest costs. Instead, we are accounting for the use of money differently, as will be explained later.

The last item that was changed, the retirement plan for the owner, could again be considered a perk or income to the owner. Therefore, that amount has been reduced in the adjustment column to zero. The new profit for the year, consequently, instead of being $26,830 is now $25,030.

Because the value of tangible assets is relatively small in this particular business, no further adjustments need to be made to the net income; therefore, the excess earnings and the adjusted net income for the year are essentially the same number, so we have shown them the same at $25,030.

Now let's look at Examples 3 and 4, the balance sheet and the income statement for **Harbor Locksmiths, Inc.** This balance sheet presents an entirely different situation. The assets are very substantial; the merchandise is worth close to a quarter of a million dollars (at cost); receivables are $55,000, and the business has liabilities of $61,578. The net worth of this business is $277,940.

Harbor Lock Example 3

HARBOR LOCKSMITHS, INC.

Balance Sheet at December 31, 1990

Assets

		Adjusted
CURRENT ASSETS:		
Cash in Bank	36,779	
Accounts Receivable	55,001	
Merchandise Inventory	241,891	
Prepaid Expenses	1,552	
TOTAL CURRENT ASSETS	335,223	
fIXED ASSETS:		
Furniture and Fixtures	24,750	
Less Accumulated Depreciation	20,455	
TOTAL FIXED ASSETS	4,295	
TOTAL ASSETS	339,518	

Liabilities and Capital

CURRENT LIABILITIES:		
Accounts Payable	27,394	
Accrued Taxes and Expenses	34,184	
TOTAL CURRENT LIABILITIES	61,578	
CAPITAL:		
Capital Stock, 1000 Shares	5,000	
Paid in Capital	54,000	
Retained Earnings	218,940	
TOTAL CAPITAL	277,940	277,940
TOTAL LIABILITIES AND CAPITAL	339,518	

Harbor Lock Example 4

HARBOR LOCKSMITHS, INC.

Statement of Income and Related Earnings
For the year ending December 31, 1990

Assets

			Adjusted
REVENUES	508,115		
Less – COST OF SALE	238,565		
GROSS PROFIT ON SALES	269,550		
Less – EXPENSES			
Salaries Office	64,115		
Salaries Owner	80,000	→	55,000
Taxes	14,054		
Office Expenses	4,564		
Repair and Maintenance	1,577		
Rent	15,385	→	25,000
Telephone	12,662		
Insurance	2,389		
Advertising	14,662	→	13,862
Legal and Accounting	2,470		
Utilities	11,763		
Auto Expenses	13,447	→	7,947
Interest Expense	4,800	→	0
Depreciation Expense	1,786	→	800
TOTAL EXPENSES	243,674		216,203
NET INCOME FOR THE YEAR	25,876		53,347
LOST INTEREST ON NET WORTH			30,573
EXCESS EARNINGS			22,779

Looking at Example 4, which is the "P and L" or income statement for the year ended December 31, 1990, we see a similar situation to the previous example in that certain adjustments need to be made in the expenses for valuation purposes. The previous owner has allocated to himself a salary of $80,000. In your view, a fair compensation to the owner for the time, effort, and the skill level is $55,000, so the change is made on the income statement worksheet as indicated with an arrow.

Another adjustment is rent. The lease is currently expiring, and the rent will be going up from about $15,000 to $25,000. This kind of situation highlights an important point often missed by prospective buyers. Some expenses from the past year's statements are sure to increase in the current year. These items should be so adjusted, just as we have done here with rent.

Advertising was adjusted downward (added back to owner compensation) by $800. The seller placed an $800 ad in a charity yearbook, not to bring in business, but to help out the organization. This was not essential to running the company.

The next adjustment in this situation, as in the previous example, involves auto expenses. Again, the company has been providing the owner with the use of an automobile, and that benefit (or perk) has been deducted from the expenses.

As in the last example, we have adjusted interest expense to zero. Your interest expense, or cost of money, will be accounted for and explained later.

Also, we have adjusted depreciation from $1786 to $800. Depreciation is usually listed on the income statement as a number that is allowed by the IRS (for tax purposes). Instead of using the depreciation figure on that statement, we use a number that more accurately reflects the amount that tangible assets will decrease in value over the year. While this is a judgment call, it is better to use judgment for valuation purposes than it is to rely on the statement's depreciation figures, that were most likely computed to get the maximum tax advantage.

With all these adjustments, the net income for the year, instead of being $25,878, is $53,347.

At this point, another very important adjustment must be made that was not an issue in the previous example. In order to operate in the same mode in which it has been operating in recent years, **Harbor Locksmiths, Inc.**, has to maintain a very substantial net worth. That is, it has to tie up capital as cash in the bank, accounts receivable, inventory, and so on.

All this adds up to $277,940. If you buy the firm, in order to keep that kind of substantial net worth, you'll either have to borrow the money and put it into the business, or use your own funds. If you borrow the $277,940, you will have to pay interest on it. If you use your own money, you will be losing interest that you would have otherwise earned by keeping it in the bank or investing it elsewhere. Therefore, in order to get a fair figure for the excess earnings, the net income has to be reduced by the interest loss.

Assuming a bank would charge at the rate of 11%, the loss would then be 11% of $277,940 or $30,573. That amount has to be deducted from the net income in order to find the appropriate excess earnings for this business. If we deduct the $30,573 from the $53,347, we arrive at the excess earnings figure of $22,774.

- **The Earnings Multiplier**

   There are a number of factors that will have impact upon the future of a business. The factors that are generally considered for valuation purposes are competitiveness, the industry as a whole, risk, the performance of the firm being valued relative to the industry, industry and company growth projections, and the desirability or appeal of the business.

   Each of these factors is rated on a scale of 1 to 6. A higher number means a better rating (6 is best and 1 is worst). Ratings are based upon subjective judgment, upon industry projections, and upon industry performance statistics. All the items used in setting the multiplier are assigned a number separately; then all the numbers are averaged. Your analysis of the excess earnings for **Nurse Care, Inc.** might work as follows:

Competitiveness (based on buyer's judgment)	4.00
Industry (based on recent industry projections as reported by U.S. Department of Commerce)	4.00
Risk (based on industry characteristics as reported by U.S. Department of Commerce, and buyer judgment)	3.00
Company (based on comparing company financial performance to industry statistics from Robert Morris Associates)	3.00
Growth (based on recent industry projections as reported by U.S. Department of Commerce)	1.50
Desirability (based on buyer judgment of the attractiveness and appeal of the industry)	3.00

Average factor   3.08
(average of above is the calculated
multiplier)

A warning here is that there is nothing cast in stone regarding the multiplier. Different people will have different opinions, not only about items like desirability, but also about the interpretation of projections, competitive strengths, and so on. Nevertheless, using a system like this does makes the valuation process more objective, and provides some criteria based rationale for setting a value and ultimately for defending the reasonableness of an offering price.

- **Putting it all Together**

We have now learned how to figure out the excess earnings for the company. We have also learned how to calculate a reasonable multiplier. Now let's look again at the original formula (Value = Net Worth + Goodwill) and apply it to the two sample businesses.

Nurses Care, Inc.

Nurses Care, Inc. is a small operation which has been in existence for eight years. Its staff includes the owner plus two assistants in the office. It's in the business of providing temporary nursing and related personnel to hospitals, clinics, and nursing homes. For purposes of this valuation, we'll assume that you are buying the company complete; that is, you will buy the cash in the bank, the accounts receivable, and the furniture and fixtures. You will also assume the payables and other liabilities.

As a practical matter, buyers usually don't buy the cash in the bank. They may or may not buy the accounts receivable. But for the sake of simplicity, we'll assume that you are buying the entire business, lock-stock-and-barrel. We will then make whatever adjustments are needed for those items that are either not bought or bought in addition to what is stated on the balance sheet.

The net worth of the company, according to the balance sheet (Example 1), is $6,524. The multiplier calculated above is 3.08. The computation is now straight-forward. The value of the business is the net worth, of $6,524, plus 3.08 times the excess earnings.

     GOODWILL = MULTIPLIER x EXCESS EARNINGS
therefore
     GOODWILL = 3.08 x $25,030 = $77,092.40
and
     VALUE = NET WORTH + GOODWILL
therefore
     VALUE = $6,524 + $77,092.40 = $83,616.40

Remember that this figure is not engraved in stone. It should be used as a guide. What this number says is that if the seller wants $150,000 for this business and will not budge, walk away from the deal. On the other hand, if the seller is asking $60,000, grab your check book and close the deal.

Now let's examine your other option, **Harbor Locksmiths, Inc.** This business has been in existence for over forty years. It has evolved into a substantial outfit that has many good corporate accounts. These accounts include hospitals, real estate companies, and engineering firms. Because of these high quality accounts, it can command a rather high hourly rate for emergency service. It does have to maintain a very substantial inventory, approximately $240,000 at cost, in order to be competitive and to be ready for customer needs for a variety of door fasteners, hinges, security systems, etc.

The net worth of this business, the assets minus the liabilities, is $277,940. In this case, we'll assume the multiplier to be four. This is not an unreasonable multiplier for a well established and profitable business. If we use the formulas (Value = Net Worth + Goodwill) and (Goodwill = Multiplier x Excess Earnings) we see that the value of the business is ($277,940 + [4 x $22,774]). If we do the arithmetic we get a total value of $369,036 as illustrated below.

GOODWILL = MULTIPLIER x EXCESS EARNINGS
therefore
GOODWILL = 4 x $22,774 = $91,096
and
VALUE = NET WORTH + GOODWILL
therefore
VALUE = $277,940 + $91,096 = $369,036

So what this tells us is that the business is worth approximately $370,000 assuming that you will buy all the assets including the cash in the bank, the accounts receivable, the inventory, and so on.

If, as is usual, you do not buy the cash in the bank, that amount ($36,779) would be deducted from the price. Also, if the receivables are to be excluded from the sale, the price should be reduced by $55,000, and so on. For purposes of computing the value of the business, we are assuming that the business is bought as a going entity with its receivables and cash. Also, we are assuming that you will take over the liabilities. Of course if liabilities are to be paid by the seller, that amount must be added back to the selling price.

The primary reason for making these assumptions is that when computing the excess earnings, it is important that the interest be computed on a going business basis. You will have to maintain a similar balance sheet with comparable receivables, payables, cash, and other assets and liabilities. Maintaining that balance sheet will mean tying money up, either your own money or borrowed money, in the business. If it is borrowed money, this will cost you the interest on the loan. If it is your own money, it will cost you the interest lost, because that money could have been invested elsewhere at prevailing rates. This interest lost is sometimes referred to as *opportunity cost.*

More on the Excess Earnings Method of Valuation

To further demonstrate this popular method of valuing a small business, we are including another example of its application in the Appendix. That second example is a computer assisted report that uses essentially the same method but with a few differences in calculation. Specifically:

- The example above assumes that the business is bought including cash and receivables, and that the buyer takes over all liabilities. The example in the appendix assumes that the seller retains cash and receivables; only specified assets are part of the transaction. Further, in the appendix example the seller retains responsibility for all liabilities.

- The first example uses an interest rate of 11%. The Appendix example uses consumer price index plus 4 points which computes to about 9.4% as of this writing. This too will have an effect on the calculation. The logic of this method of computing cost of money is explained within the sample report.

What if the Valuation Result is a Negative Number?

In some instances, the value calculated by this method will be either a negative number, or a number that is less than the fair market value of the tangible assets. If, for example, the owner is earning a total compensation (salary and profits) of $10,000 per year, and a reasonable salary based upon the work involved is $30,000 per year, the excess earnings figure will be negative. The fact is that a business in this situation is not a financially rational investment, if it is to be run as a free standing enterprise. The owner is, in a sense, giving up money for the privilege of keeping the business going (not all that unusual of a small business situation).

A negative number for excess earnings does indicate that the business being valued is not a good stand-alone investment. If you are buying a business in the hope of running it on a turnkey basis, it is best to stay away from a firm with negative earnings unless you have reason to believe that the profit picture will turn around quickly and dramatically. If you do buy a business in this situation with the plan of developing it, pay no more than the fair market value of its assets. The excess earnings figure, when multiplied by the multiplier is mathematically exacerbated. This does not really make practical sense, especially when you consider that the better the multiplier, the higher the negative value will be. If the value calculated by this method is less than zero, assume the turnkey value of the business to be the value of the tangible assets.

A Word about Asset Value

As you know, asset value as indicated on the balance sheet and the fair market value of assets can be two very different things. In buying a business, assets should be valued and transacted at fair market value. In some instances buyer and seller can agree upon a fair market value. In other instances, an outside appraiser must be called in to render an opinion as to fair market value.

Be sure to adjust the net worth on the balance sheet based upon fair market rather than stated (depreciated) value, before computing cost of money based upon net worth.

Cash Flow Method

Another common way to valuate a business is by determining how much of a loan the cash flow will support. That is, to look at the profits and add back to profits any expense for depreciation and amortization. To use this method first adjust owner's salary to a fair salary or at least a marginally acceptable salary for yourself if you will be running the company. If the new salary is lower than the current owner's salary, the difference will be added to cash flow. If the new salary is higher than the current owner's salary, the difference will be subtracted from cash flow for valuation purposes. In using this method you may also subtract from cash flow an estimated annual amount for equipment replacement.

The adjusted cash flow number is used as a benchmark to measure the firm's ability to service debt. If the adjusted cash flow is, for example, $10,000, and prevailing interest rates are 12%, and the buyer wants to amortize the loan over 3 years, the maximum value of the firm would be about $25,300. This is the loan payment that $10,000 would support amortized over 3 years on a monthly basis.

This method is pragmatic, but a bit illogical. It is pragmatic in that it dictates the amount that you can borrow and repay without getting yourself into a negative cash flow situation. If you need the salary and or cash flow from the business being bought, you simply can not afford to sustain a negative cash flow.

However, the cash flow method is flawed for two reasons. First, a price that is not justified by this method based on, say a two year payback period, may well be justified based on a five or ten year payback. The number of years chosen, then, is somewhat arbitrary, from a price and value point of view. Further, some buyers subtract the amount of cash they have available as a down payment from the loan amount which, of course, can make a very big difference in the computation and can further contribute to the arbitrary nature of the outcome. Note, however, that the cash flow method may not be arbitrary at all in the circumstance of a lender insisting on a maximum number of years to retire the loan, or creating other conditions such that a price must be justified based upon this method. In this situation, logical or not, the cash flow method dictates the amount that you can pay for a business.

Second, a seller will justifiably argue that the business will retain its value and be salable at the end of the amortization period. Therefore, debt service should be figured using a number closer to interest only, as is typically done in real estate analysis or in analyzing investment securities (publicly traded stocks and bonds).

We recommend that buyers calculate projected cash flow and compare that with their own financial needs. However, despite its practicality in determining whether a business is affordable, this is not a great method for computing a fair value for a company.

Tangible Assets (Balance Sheet) Method

In some instances, a business is worth no more than the value of its tangible assets. This would be the case for many businesses that are losing money or paying the owner(s) less than a fair market compensation. Generally, buying a business based on this method should be limited to a company buying another firm in the same business where the assets have immediate value, or to someone buying the assets with a very clear plan as to how to use those assets.

Some intangibles such as patents or copyrights might have value to the right buyer. We were recently involved in the sale of a scuba diving school that was in a break-even situation. The company owned a copyright to a video on diving that was in distribution and earning royalty income from the distributor. While the company itself sold for the value of its tangible assets, the owners were delighted to accept a separate offer of $17,000 for the copyright. The buyer, who owned a company in the film distribution business, looked at the anticipated earnings from the video, and applied a capitalized earnings formula to it. He calculated that the $17,000 investment would earn about $10,000 for each of the next three years, and then would be worthless. That means he would earn a net $13,000 ($30,000 − 17,000 = $13,000), which is better than a 20% return on an annualized basis.

Cost to Create Approach (Leapfrog Start-up)

Sometimes companies or individuals will purchase a company just to avoid the difficulties of starting from scratch (see Chapter IV). You may reason (quite correctly) that a startup takes time and money. Following this line of reasoning it may be justified to pay a premium of 10% or 15% above the sum of projected start up costs due to the time and effort that you will save.

As a practical matter, this approach is not very common and is a bit dangerous. A profitable business is worth more than this approach will justify. A business that is not profitable may have flaws that should discourage its purchase. If you bought this kind of business, you would be inheriting those flaws such as bad location, bad reputation, production problems, etc. Its primary use is in situations where no other method is appropriate, or in combination with other methods of valuation.

Rules of Thumb Methods

Many people are convinced that there are some quick rules of thumb that could determine the value of a business. Some of these rules of thumb state, for example, that an insurance agency is worth 1.5 times annual commissions, or that a gas station is worth 20 cents times the number of gallons sold in the past year. These formulas may indeed be fair averages, but they give very little help in determining the value of a particular business.

The problem with rule of thumb formulas is that they are statistically derived from the sale of many businesses of each type. That is, an organization might compile statistics on perhaps 100 gas stations that were sold over a three year period. They will then average all the selling prices and calculate that the average gas station sold for an amount equivalent to 20 cents per gallon pumped in a one year period. The rule of thumb is thus created. However, some stations may have sold for 10 cents per gallon pumped while other may have sold for 40 cents per gallon pumped in a year.

The rule of thumb averages may be accurate for the business whose performance is right about at the average. The business with expenses and profits that are right on target with industry averages may well sell for a price in line with the rule of thumb formula. Others will vary. To apply the rule of thumb to a business that varies significantly from the average is not appropriate.

Nevertheless, industry averages can be a good *quick and dirty* starting point to valuation. Check with industry associations(s) for rule of thumb formulas for buying a business. The Appendix contains a source for further information on rule of thumb formulas. Before taking any rule of thumb formula too seriously, check to see how closely your firm's financial performance stacks up to the industry averages. Sources to examine industry averages may also be available from your trade association(s). Other sources are listed in the Appendix.

Value of Specific Intangible Assets

This is an often overlooked approach to valuation. Yet in some cases, especially companies acquiring other companies, it is the only appropriate approach that will result in a sale. The approach is based upon the buyer's buying a wanted intangible asset versus creating it. Many times buying can be a cost efficient and time saving alternative.

For example, we recently sold a temporary employment agency. This agency specialized in matching people with certain computer skills with organizations that temporarily needed those skills. Because there was a shortage of these workers in the area where the selling company did business, placing workers was not difficult. However, finding qualified workers was very difficult.

We approached firms in the same or related businesses. Through our research, we calculated that recruiting a qualified worker costs an agency at least $200. Therefore, we asked a price of $175.00 for each worker in the pool of available employees.

To the buyer, this not only saved $25.00 per worker, but it also cut down on the time it took to recruit. The overhead of the selling company was not an issue because the buying company already had the system in place that the overhead expense was paying for (offices, computer system, phones, etc.). In fact, whether the seller was making or losing money was of little consequence to the buyer. The value to the buyer was the value of buying a qualified worker versus recruiting a worker through the more traditional methods of advertising, interviewing, etc.

A common application of this method is the acquisition of a customer base in a company to company acquisition. Customers with a high likelihood of being retained are valuable in most industries. Examples of industries where companies are bought and sold based upon the value of the customer base include insurance agencies, advertising agencies, payroll services, and bookkeeping services.

If you plan to buy a business primarily for its customer base, insist on a credit for each customer that is not retained for a stated period of time. For example, you may want to offer $100 per customer but with a pro-rated credit for each customer that leaves during the twelve months following the closing of the sale. Pro-rating is based upon when the customer leaves — if a customer leaves after 6 months, for example, half of the $100 would be returned to you.

Chapter Summary

There is no surefire way to value a company for buying and selling purposes. Ultimately, the value of a company is the perceived value to a buyer who is ready, willing, and able to buy it. However, there are a number of approaches to estimating value; some of those are discussed above. For a stand-alone, or turnkey business acquisition, the excess earnings approach is generally the preferred method of valuation. When making an offer, it can be helpful to be prepared to demonstrate the reasonableness of that offer based upon a recognized valuation method.

VIII Evaluating an Acquisition beyond the Financial Statements

Much of what you need to know to make a decision on purchasing a business is contained in its current and past financial statements. However, financial statements do not tell the entire story. There are several things to watch for and to examine that are either not part of a financial statement, or are at best indicated by those statements. Financial statements tell much about a firm's past; but you are really interested in its future.

Accountants and other financial professionals will warn you not to consider purchasing a company without closely analyzing its financial statements. We would not for a second disagree with this advice. However, we will add that it is equally as foolish to rely solely on a company's financial statements to make a buy/no buy decision. Before buying, there is more you need to know about than a company's past financial performance.

Some of the recommended non-financial evaluation steps are outlined in this section.

Cash Off The Top (Skimming)

The situation often comes up in which a business owner will maintain that he earns a lot more than he reports to the government. No doubt this is often true. The question is, should you as a buyer pay a premium for cash coming off the top, based on the owner's say so? In general the answer is no. In all cases if a buyer is making claims of cash off the top, proceed with extreme caution. Some experts counsel that if a seller is cheating the government, he is probably cheating you too. While this argument is a bit simplistic, the point is a valid one.

Some people who are sophisticated in buying cash businesses, use a number of analytical techniques to estimate just how much is coming off the top. For example, experienced laundromat buyers will look closely at utility bills to determine approximate machine usage and derive a sales volume estimate from that information. Buyers of retail stores will look at the store's prices and wholesale costs, and then look at the gross sales and cost of goods sold figures on the firm's tax return. If, for example, you know a store's markup policy and its cost of goods sold, you can estimate true sales and profit figures from those numbers. If a store consistently sets price by doubling the amount it pays for each item, the gross sales figure should be double the cost of goods sold. In any case, if you are considering the purchase of a cash business, it is a good idea to *work the business* (actually stay on the premises all day, posing as an employee) for a week or two weeks to get a hands-on measure of actual sales volume.

It is never advisable to take a seller's word for it if he or she claims cash is coming off the top. Such a claim is at least a clue to the owner's character, and should signal caution. We have had people with books indicating net income well under $20,000 tell us they are really earning six figure incomes on a regular basis. Our reaction to outlandish claims such as these has been to not get involved. First of all, we don't want to be in the position of helping to convince a buyer that this is a profitable business when we don't know that to be the case. Secondly, we are immediately suspect of a seller who is claiming to cheat the government on such a grandiose scale, and we prefer not to do business with people who we don't trust. Finally, we are afraid that if the claims are true, and if the owner is routinely so willing to tell people, the IRS may come in at any time and close down the operation.

New and Pending Legislation

When we were new to business brokering, we listed a medical temporary employment service. The business recruited nurses and nurses aids, and offered their services to hospitals and other health care facilities. The financial statements were picture perfect — a solid upward trend, with current owner compensation (profit and salary) approaching $500,000 per year. The statements were CPA audited, leaving little doubt as to their accuracy. We thought that at the asking price of $1,000,000 this would be an easy sale.

We first presented the business to a larger company in a neighboring state. The vice president looked at the financials and was impressed. He then asked about pending state legislation regarding nurse temporary agencies. He went on to explain that in Massachusetts, where his company was located, recent legislation severely cut into profits of most agencies. We went back and looked into pending legislation and found that sure enough, there was a bill before the legislature modeled after the Massachusetts bill. Further, we talked to people in the business and were told that either the pending bill or one like it was expected to pass within months. We now knew that this million dollar listing was overpriced based on this new information.

Now we know enough to check on possible legal changes that can affect a business before offering it for sale. You should be aware of legal situations that can be expected to impact a business, before making an offer to purchase. Ask the owner, others in the industry, industry associations, your state legislator(s), or your lawyer. This kind of eventuality will not show up on a financial statement, no matter how carefully it is scrutinized. A seller or his representative may not know about or may be purposely hiding it — it is up to you to find out.

Don't overlook the fact that legal changes can work both ways. That is, they can have a positive effect on some types of companies. For example, a large conglomerate recently purchased a medium size firm that manufactures insulated electrical cable. The target firm was surviving but struggling. The type of insulation used for its cabling did not meet electrical code in many areas, making sales impossible, except in those few areas that accepted this kind of insulation.

However, the large company knew that another firm that manufactured the same kind of cable was engaged in an all out campaign to convince local authorities that this cabling was absolutely safe. This campaign was meeting with a lot of success. The acquiring company reasoned that it could acquire the target firm, and reap the benefits of the campaign that its competitor was paying for. The campaign to change electrical code would expand the market for all players, not just the campaign's sponsor.

The point is to be aware of legislative and related issues that can have a powerful impact on a business. Laws and legislation can and do ruin businesses and propel others from mediocrity to success. Such changes can dwarf the relevance of historical financial data.

Societal and Lifestyle Changes that Can Impact a Company

Attitudes, lifestyles, likes, and dislikes are ever changing. Many of these changes can have significant impacts on businesses. Spotting societal trends soon enough can lead to substantial profits for those willing to risk money on the trend that they recognize. Likewise, failing to recognize an important trend can be costly.

For example, the past few years have ushered in a new concern for our environment. As people become aware of the potential damage to the earth and atmosphere, certain habits and attitudes are changing. About two years ago the owner of the only local diaper delivery company in this area offered to sell the business to his manager for $50,000 and offered to finance 50% of the deal. The manager declined. Today, a number of parents are switching from disposable diapers to cloth diapers because of concerns that disposables are environmentally harmful. Diaper delivery services are the obvious beneficiary. The manager who turned down the offer is probably kicking himself for his decision. The owner recently received an unsolicited $200,000 offer for the company.

Just as in the section above on legal changes, nothing in the financial statements would indicate positive or negative societal trends. Nevertheless societal trends can have a powerful impact, either positive or negative.

New Competition

In our free market system, competition is a fact of life. It is a normal part of the business environment. However there are situations where changes in the competitive environment can have an unusually severe impact on a business.

Last year we received a call from the owner of a very successful natural food store. He asked if we could meet to discuss the sale of his store. This surprised us because we spoke with him a few months earlier, and he had expressed no interest in selling. At the meeting, he told us that business was going well, and the new health awareness could only help his business. We asked him why he changed his mind and wanted to sell now. He offered only a vague response.

After our meeting we asked friends who were natural food enthusiasts if they had heard any news about natural food marketing in this area. One person said, "Sure, haven't you heard? A supermarket size natural food store is opening in town." When we asked where it would be located, we knew that we had found the answer. The new store was to open about a half mile from the store that was looking to sell.

Had a buyer bought this heretofore successful natural food store based upon past financial performance, that buyer would have been in for an unpleasant surprise. This new competitor was more than the kind of competition that most small retailers learn to deal with. This was a huge store with big dollars for advertising, lower prices due to massive buying power, and a stellar reputation both as a champion of the cause of natural food, and as a successful business.

Incidentally, we refused to list the business because the owner refused to disclose the plans of the new competitor to a prospective buyer. Within 8 months of our meeting, he filed for bankruptcy. The new natural food supermarket had quite literally put him out of business.

Competition, the Long View

In evaluating competition, it is important to avoid taking too narrow a view. You must look not only at direct competitors but also at indirect competitors. For example, a video producer may consider only other video producers to be competition, while a toy store owner may consider only other toy stores as competitors.

This view of competition is too narrow because it defines competition from the perspective of the business. Competition should be defined from the perspective of the customer. For example, suppose you are an aunt or uncle taking care of your six year old nephew for a Saturday afternoon. You have budgeted twenty five dollars to spend for entertaining your six year old charge. You offer him several recreational choices such as a movie, roller skating, an amusement park, a museum, or a visit to a toy store with a purchase of up to the twenty five dollar limit.

From your perspective (or more to the point, from your nephew's perspective) the movie, roller skating rink, amusement park, and museum are all competitors of the toy store for your dollars. As a prospective business buyer, being aware of the competition in a broader sense will lead to a more far reaching pre-purchase evaluation.
For another example, recall the temporary medical employment agency discussed in the subsection above (New and Pending Legislation). That company offers workers the flexibility of working only when they want to work. This policy helps them attract qualified workers because it is a real advantage since health care facilities typically require rotating shifts that require full time and some weekend hours.

Now this agency is losing its advantage because the health care facilities, tired of paying premium prices for staff from temporary agencies, are in effect setting up their own in-house agencies. That is, workers can apply to work through the in-house pool, meaning the facility offers no guarantee of work on any day, nor do the workers guarantee availability. This is essentially the same arrangement as that offered by the agency. It comprises competition from a new and heretofore unexpected source — the customer. Only a prospective buyer taking the long view of competition could have anticipated this source of competition.

Outdated Facilities

Be careful about buying a business that has production or office equipment that is inefficient by modern standards. If another company has equipment that will do the job better and or cheaper, the firm with the outdated equipment may eventually find itself at a competitive disadvantage, resulting in a gradual atrophy of business.

Even if your equipment is dated but the competition has equally dated equipment, this too can be dangerous. The competition may upgrade forcing you to do the same or lose business. Or, a new competitor may emerge reasoning that an opportunity exists because others in the industry are using dated and inefficient equipment.

We are not implying that a company must buy every new piece of equipment that shows up on the market. That equipment only has an economic justification if it will lead to better product, lower cost, or new business. Buying new equipment without economic justification is no slower a route to business problems than is operating with outdated facilities.

Economic Sensitivities

Some businesses are relatively immune to cyclical economic changes. A pharmacy, for example, is little affected by economic booms, recessions, upturns, or downturns. A sick person needs medicine regardless of the economy.

Many businesses, though, are subject to the vagaries of the economy. New car dealers and building contractors tend to do well in a good economy, poorly in a slow economy. In a recession, auto repair and shoe repair businesses thrive — when money is limited, repair is more affordable than replacement. If the economy is in transition, be very careful about making projections based upon past financials for businesses that can be expected to change for better or worse with the economy.

To get an indication of how a business may perform under different economic environments, you can examine industry projections from trade associations, stock brokerages, or other sources. To examine how an industry has performed previously during different economic conditions sec Business Statistics 1961-1988, published by the U.S. Department of Commerce. Finding industry projections and other industry data is discussed in the next section of this chapter. Complete references to specific sources can be found in the Appendix.

Other elements to watch for, that won't show up on financial statements, are covered elsewhere in this book. For example, Chapter IX (Companies Buying Companies) details company to company acquisitions. In these instances, synergies may be more important than a target's financial performance as a stand alone company.

In Chapter IV, the section called *Diamonds In the Rough* includes discussion of under-performing companies that can be easily turned around with the right combination of skill and circumstance.

Industry Information

An important part of your pre-acquisition evaluation should involve researching the industry that you plan to enter. You also should check into the industry(s) that supply your target business, and if your target business sells to other businesses, the industry situation of its customers. This industry research is as easy to access as it is important. Yet many buyers skip this important pre-purchase step.

This section will outline the kinds of information that you should be looking for, several of the appropriate sources of business information, and the steps you will need to take to find the information.

- **Goals of the Research**

  In researching your target company's industry, your goal is to learn the answers to a few broad questions:

  - What are the industry's prospects for the future?
  - How is your target company performing relative to other companies in the same industry?
  - What is the current status of major supplier industries? Are there any indicated problems or opportunities that would have a bearing on the target company? (For example are supply shortages, price changes, or new products expected?)

  If your target company relies on business to business sales;

  - What is the current status and projected future of customer industries? Are there any indications of increases or decreases in their needs that could affect the target business? For example, suppose that you are considering the purchase of a company that sells sugar to the soft drink industry. If soft drink industry projections indicate that sales of soda with sugar are expected to decrease, this kind of information could adversely affect your target company.

- **Finding Information**

  The amount of good reliable information that is available to the public for free or at nominal cost is mind boggling. While it may seem that finding the required information noted above would be difficult, in most cases it is quite easy, although a little time consuming. Much of the information can be found in a major public library or a business college library. Visit a nearby public or college library and ask if they have the information that you need. You don't even have to know exactly which books or periodicals you need; the reference librarian can help translate your information needs into specific sources. If the library you visit does not have what you need, the librarian may be able to direct you to a library that does.

Other information is available from private sources, trade and industry associations, the U.S. Government, and state and local governments. A few information sources are listed below with a brief description. More sources of information can be found in the Appendix (Sources of Further Information).

Industry Statistics, Projections, and General Information

You will first want to check into the industry itself, learning about its recent past, its current status both in terms of opportunities and problems, and its projected future. It is also important that you learn about industry practices and standards. Some sources are listed and described below:

• **Trade and Industry Associations**

Just about every industry, trade, and profession in this country has at least one membership association. These associations perform varied functions. A common function is the collection and dissemination of industry statistics and other kinds of industry information.

There is a real range of quality, but many associations can supply excellent information about the industries that they service. What's more, associations will often send you piles of information for free or for a price that is hardly significant relative to the value of that information.

To find out who the association are for any industry, consult *The Encyclopedia of Associations* by **Gale Research** (see the Appendix), which is available at most full service libraries. This guide is published annually. It lists thousands of associations, along with contact names, addresses, and brief descriptions of each. Even if you think you know who the associations are for a given industry, consult this guide anyway. You might be surprised to learn about other associations that you never heard of in the same industry.

It doesn't make sense to purchase a business without getting whatever industry information is available from one of its associations. This is a recommended first step in the information gathering process.

• **Independent Industry Projections**

The only problem with information obtained from an association is that the information was prepared by or for those with a stake in that industry. There are independent sources that are well worth consulting, along with industry sources. Some of these are listed below:

U.S. Industrial Outlook, U.S. Department of Commerce

This popular annual guide is available at many libraries. It is also available from the U.S. government at a current price of $27.00 from the U.S. Superintendent of Documents (see the Appendix). It presents prospects for over 350 U.S. industries, based upon Department of Commerce data. It is well presented, authoritative information. If the industry(s) that you are looking for is covered, this guide is well worth consulting.

Standard And Poors Industry Surveys

This guide, available in major libraries, presents current status, historical data, and projections for a growing number of industries. It is continuously updated on a section by section basis. The information is generally more detailed than the *U.S. Industrial Outlook.* It too is worth a consultation.

Predicasts Forecasts

This guide is similar to *Standard And Poors Industry Surveys.* It is a bit harder to find-available only at some of the better full service or business libraries. If you can find it, it is well worth consulting along with *Standard And Poors Industry Surveys* and *U.S. Industrial Outlook.*

Stock Brokerage Firms

Some of the major full service stock brokerages offer industry evaluations for free or for a nominal charge to the public. While in most instances they will give available reports to anyone, their reason for disseminating the information is not altruism. The reports are supposed to be for investors and prospective investors to evaluate industries for possible investment opportunities. Simply call the local offices of major stock brokerages and ask if they have a report on the industry in which you are interested, and can send it to you.

Small Business Source Book, **Gale Research**

This guide is available at some major libraries. It is also available directly from the publisher (see the Appendix).

If the industry of interest is covered, *Small Business Source Book* will have lots of information that can be helpful. It explains some of the basic industry practices, and presents a number of sources from which you can get more information on an industry by industry basis.

U.S. Department of Labor Statistics

The U.S. Department of Labor Statistics puts out several publications and periodic updates that present statistics and other information on various occupations. If you are considering acquiring a business that is highly dependent on labor, especially skilled or professional labor, these publications can be helpful in your evaluation. Specifically, they can answer questions such as:

- What is the supply of labor likely to be? Will there be shortages? Will there be over-supply?
- What is the average compensation range for the needed employees?
- How rapidly are salaries expected to increase?
- Is the current owner under or overpaying based upon national averages?

Some of the Department of Labor Statistics publications are listed in the Appendix.

Specific Industry Financial Information

Along with general industry information, it would be a good idea to learn how the company that you may buy stacks up against the industry as a whole. It is not difficult to compare a firm's financial statements with those of the industry in general. For example, you can compare your target firm's profit levels with those of the industry as a whole (on a percentage of sales basis). You can just as easily examine how your target firm compares in terms of operating expenses, financial ratios such as inventory turn-over, sales/receivable, debt/worth, etc.

Suppose, for example, the financial statements for the camera store that you are considering indicate cost of goods sold to be 35%. If you learn that the industry average for cost of goods sold is 38%, this figure would probably not be cause for concern. If, however, you were to look it up and find that cost of goods for camera stores was closer to 65% on average, this would indicate the need for further investigation. Comparing a firm's financial results to industry norms can help you spot overspending, sloppy or inefficient management, and problems that if corrected can become opportunities. Some sources to find industry financial data for comparison are:

RMA Annual Statement Studies, **Robert Morris Associates**

This is the best known of the sources of industry statistics and ratios. It is by far the most common source of its type among bankers and venture capitalists. It is available at most major libraries or directly from the publisher for about $60.00 (Robert Morris Associates, 1 Liberty Place, Philadelphia, PA 19103, 215-851-0585).

Internal Revenue Service

The department of the U.S. government best known for its task as tax collector performs other services as well. One of those services involves publication of industry financial data. One such publication, *Statistics of Income, Corporation Income Tax Returns,* is published yearly but for the year two years previous to the current year. It has much of the same kinds of information as the **Robert Morris** publication. However, the IRS information is dated and not as easy to follow.

This guide is available from the **U.S. Superintendent of Documents** (see the Appendix for the address).

The IRS also publishes much more detailed financial information on an industry by industry basis. The Statistics of Income Division of the IRS publishes *Corporation Source Book, Partnership Source Book,* and *Sole Proprietorship Source Book.* These source books are available for $175, $30, and $95 respectively at current prices. However, you can buy specific pages (corresponding to specific industries) for $1.00 per page.

To order or for more information contact: Director, Statistics of Income Division, Internal Revenue Service, 1111 Constitution Avenue N.W., Washington, DC 20224.

These source books *are not* currently available from the U.S. Government Printing Office and are seldom available at libraries.

Almanac of Business and Industrial Financial Ratios, **Prentice Hall**

This resource book is published annually. It is compiled by Dr. Leo Troy from IRS data and other sources. It is a very complete and detailed guide, more so than the **Robert Morris** guide. It is available at major libraries.

Current Industry Issues

In evaluating an industry, it is always advisable to look into current articles about the industry, its prospects, and its problems. Some of the places to check include:

Trade Press

Practically every industry has at least one, and more likely, several periodicals that cover industry issues. Many of these publications are available through the industry associations (see section on trade associations, above).

Business Publications Rates and Data

Business Publications Rates and Data, published by **Standard Rate and Data Service** is an index of periodicals by industry. This guide can help you find appropriate industry publications. It is available at most good libraries.

Business Periodicals Index

Business Periodicals Index (BPI), available in most reference libraries, is a monthly guide to articles published in any of several hundred business oriented publications. Articles are listed by subject.

Wall Street Journal Index

The Wall Street Journal Index, as the name implies, is an index to *The Wall Street Journal.* As one of the most respected business publications in the world, an article in this daily paper that is relevant to your industry of interest is mandatory reading.

New York Times Index

This too is an index to a highly respected daily newspaper. It is worth checking to see if the *Times* has published anything recently about your industry of interest.

CD ROM Indexes

Many libraries are buying machines that hold huge periodical indexes on CD disks. The disks are periodically updated. They are the high tech equivalent of many periodical indexes rolled into one. Further, many (not all) of the publications that are indexed are available on a special microfilm cartridge. The reference will so indicate. Even for the most computer illiterate, this machine is easy to use, easier perhaps than the old fashioned paper indexes. One of the common CD ROM machines that many libraries use is called *InfoTrac* (made by **Information Access Company**).

Other Sources of Information

There are a number of other sources of information that can be helpful to you. Some are listed below:

* **Chambers of Commerce**

  Most localities have a local chamber of commerce. Local chambers can be an excellent source of local information such as demographics, data on important local industries, and local economic information.

- **State and Local Governments**

Most states now have a state department of economic development. A common responsibility of these departments is to collect and analyze state economic data and make it available to the public. Information is generally free or available for a nominal fee. The biggest problem with economic development offices is finding out what they have available. Most have at least state wide and local area demographics, state manufacturing directories, and information on state tourism.

- **U.S. Government**

The United States Government is the world's largest publisher. Business information includes a broad range of topics such as export information, census data, and management booklets published by the Small Business Administration. An excellent guide to government information is *Information U.S.A*, by Matthew Lesko (see the Appendix). This book details the myriad of information available and explains where and how to get it.

Note that certain U.S. libraries are designated as Federal Depository Libraries. A library so designated will have available much of what the government publishes. A Federal Depository Library is required to be open to the public free of charge. However, this requirement applies only to the government collection. Access to other library facilities can be restricted as long as government publications are freely accessible.

- **Ask the Reference Librarian**

Librarians are highly trained specialists who know how to locate information. Their services can be invaluable to you in your research efforts. What's more, public librarians will assist you at no charge. If you know the kind of information that you need but don't know where to find it, a business librarian will know. He or she will also know about the resources of other libraries and similar institutions, and about tracking down the information you need.

The only warning here is to avoid asking librarians to do your research. Their job is to point you in the right direction and to assist you as needed. It is not to do the work for you.

- **Computer Accessed Data Bases**

We are currently in the midst of a revolution in research procedure. It is now possible, and becoming increasingly practical, to do exhaustive research from virtually any computer. There are a myriad of computerized databases available to anyone with a computer and a modem.

In many ways computerized research is superior to the traditional methods. Searches can be carried out much faster. As any seasoned researcher will tell you, finding needed information sometimes involves travelling from library to library. If the researcher is not in a major metropolitan area, out of town travel is not uncommon. With computerized research, information can be hunted down right from the researcher's desk. Databases can be searched literally the world over via telephone lines.

Further, computers can more quickly pinpoint the desired information than a human being can. If, for example, you need information regarding the export of toys, computer databases allow you to search via key words and phrases. So you would tell the database to search and display only articles that contain both the key words *toy* and *export*. The computer would dutifully do this accurately and do it in mere moments. You can limit further by instructing the computer, for example, to search for *toy trucks* and *exports* to *France* or *Spain*.

The only problems with computerized databases are a) they are currently expensive to use, and b) using them efficiently takes some experience and some skill. If you are new at using on-line databases, it is easily possible to run up a bill of $50 or $75 without getting much in the way of useful information.

An industry has sprouted in recent years called information brokering. Information brokers, usually librarians by training, will perform computer searches for you for a fee. For the inexperienced researcher, this fee is usually well worth it. The broker's fee will be paid several times over in the quality of information successfully retrieved, and in money saved on database usage fees, which typically charge by the minute. An experienced information broker will know how to design a search to use as few expensive on-line minutes as possible.

If you do wish to try to search for business information on your own, we recommend that you start by subscribing to CompuServe. CompuServe is a service that allows users access to hundreds of databases. It even provides a search tool called *IQuest* which can pinpoint and access the appropriate databases for you based on your defined information needs. For subscription and other information call CompuServe at 800-848-8199.

Computerized research will probably become more prevalent, less expensive, and easier to use over the next few years. Some people even think that computerized databases will eventually antiquate traditional library research. In any case, it is already a research method that can't be ignored as a viable option for finding business information.

Chapter Summary

A firm's financial statements tell much of its past and provide a good indication of its future. Financial statements often transcend an owner's claims and an eager buyer's hunches and hopes. With rare exception (such as buying assets at fair market value and buying for precisely defined, limited goals) detailed examination of statements going back at least three years is a prerequisite to buying any company.

However, while financials tell a good deal about a company, they do not tell all. Such uncontrollable circumstances as new legislation, new competition, or economic transitions can create problems or opportunities not indicated by the statements.

There are many sources available to anyone who wants to look into an industry, as well as the factors that may be affecting it. Projections, industry averages, and information on industry issues are all available with a bit of digging. Some of the sources and research procedures are outlined in this chapter. Finally, the research method of "asking around in the community," should not be ignored.

IX Companies Buying Companies

For going businesses, large and small, acquiring a company can be an effective shortcut to growth. Acquiring is faster, less risky, cheaper, and easier to finance than are traditional growth strategies. What's more, in a well executed acquisition, the acquiring company can take advantage of *synergies*. That is, the two companies together will be stronger and more profitable than either company was previously.

The Concept of Synergy

Synergy is roughly defined as two or more things together being better or more effective than the sum of their parts. As it's used here, it means two or more companies merging such that the combined resources of the merged unit have more than the sum of the value they had individually.

For example, suppose XYZ Engineering Company has very skilled sales and marketing people. Through their marketing abilities they have a number of contracts for sophisticated engineering projects. However, their engineering staff leaves something to be desired. The engineers are inexperienced and are not well equipped to handle the contracts that XYZ sales personnel are able to secure.

ABC Engineering Company has opposite strengths and weaknesses. This firm is made up of top flight engineers. However ABC does not have strong marketing abilities, so it holds few contracts despite its engineering superiority to XYZ. The obvious solution — merge ABC and XYZ into one company. XYZ's marketing staff could secure contracts, while ABC's engineers could complete the jobs.

While this example is simple, it demonstrates a powerful business concept that is being exercised all the time by companies of all sizes. Some of this nation's most successful firms owe their success largely to *growth through acquisition* or *external growth* strategies.

Growth through acquisition is often a quicker path to achieving a business goal than are other methods. Conventional wisdom is that growth comes gradually through delivering quality products and services, and effectively marketing those products and services. While this is one effective means to growth, it is not the only one. Another way to add customers, leads, production capabilities, and other intangible assets is to buy them.

Here are a few of the ways that companies can take advantage of synergies through acquisition:

- **Exploiting Distribution Channels**

  A natural marketing goal of acquisition is the merging and sharing of distribution channels. A distribution channel, or more to the point, a customer base, typically takes years of hard work to develop. However, acquisition can be a very effective shortcut as is demonstrated in the examples below:

A distributor of outdoor furniture, which we'll call *Yard and Patio Furniture Co.* had been selling its products to garden and patio retailers for over 15 years. The company's owner wanted to expand. He was familiar with the tried and true methods of growing a business; he had been using them for 15 years. In the past he had grown by hiring sales people to knock on doors, advertising by direct mail, and more recently using telemarketing. All of the methods worked to some degree, but involved risking time and money.

With our help, the owner looked at the alternative possibility of growth through acquisition. He decided that the purchase of a company was worth considering. Together we set the following acquisition goals for the company: a) add a new product line(s) that could be sold to *Yard and Patio's* current customer base; b) add a new customer base for *Yard and Patio's* line of outdoor furniture; c) increase *Yard and Patio's* sales and profits, without a corresponding increase in overhead.

After a period of six months of looking, this firm found and bought a company that imports specialized planters and wholesales them to garden and patio shops. Now *Yard and Patio Furniture* can sell its furniture to the selling company's customers, and sell the selling company's planters to its own furniture customers. The two companies were geographically far enough apart that there was very little overlap in customers.

In another example, a large company owned a regional (west coast) manufacturing firm that made plumbing fixtures for mobile homes. It purchased a midwestern manufacturer of mobile home heating devices. Of course, both companies sold to the same industry, mobile home manufacturers, but in different geographic regions. The goals here were to instantly gain a midwest distribution channel for the west coast company, and a west coast channel for the midwest firm. Now this firm is selling plumbing and heating devices in both the west and midwest by exploiting its pre-existing and its acquired distribution channels. The company is now trying to find and purchase similar firms in other regions to expand further, using the same synergistic strategy.

In both of these instances, developing new customers by relying on the traditional bag of tricks of sales and marketing would have been a far more cumbersome, expensive, and time consuming undertaking than was the path chosen. In fact in the case of the mobile home component example, the acquired company nearly doubled its volume overnight through the acquisition. The buying company has gone from a 300 million dollar firm ten years ago to a 1.2 billion dollar firm today, primarily through its *synergistic external growth strategy.*

•   **Economies of Scale**

It is a well accepted business principle that as volume of sales increase, expenses as a percentage of sales decrease. *Fixed expenses* such as rent, salaries, insurance, etc., don't change with every additional sale the way *variable expenses* do. Taking advantage of economies of scale is a clear and common reason for one company to acquire or merge with another company.

For example, the owner of a small payroll service company reasoned that his company would be most efficient when its volume was near the capacity of the mini-computer it owned. After all, the computer costs were pretty much the same whether the machine was at 1% or 98% of capacity. Further, the company could grow by about 25% without adding any new personnel, and could grow to the capacity of the computer by adding only two full time employees. To take advantage of these and other economies of scale, the owner set a growth goal of 100% over one and one-half years. He expected that this ambitious goal would take not only time, but also sales effort, and money. The original plan was to add a full time sales person and to use extensive direct mail advertising to area businesses.

Rather than develop new customers through the usual methods, this firm took advantage of an opportunity to essentially buy customers. It did so by purchasing a company with 60 active payroll accounts. This brought the buying company 2/3 of the way to its goal as soon as the deal was closed. What's more, the buyer anticipated reaching break even in one year; a full 33% faster than the 18 months needed by the originally planned method of growth.

It didn't matter to the buyer that the selling firm was barely breaking even. The two firms could merge and take advantage of synergies. The buyer sold off the selling company's computer and laid off one of its two employees. Further, the buyer eventually moved the seller's whole operation into his existing facility, thereby saving on rent and related expenses. Clearly, the newly merged firm enjoyed significant economies of scale which showed up dramatically on the bottom line.

- **Production Capabilities/Competitive Advantages**

Sometimes one firm will acquire another to gain access to production capabilities, proprietary processes or patented processes, favorable locations, or favorable supply contracts. Recall the example from Chapter IV, of a computer peripheral manufacturing company that bought a small software company, primarily to gain access to the seller's proprietary software. Had the peripheral firm not been able to buy the software company, it would have had to hire programmers to develop appropriate software at a much higher cost.

- **Synergistic Products**

A company that is successfully marketing a product or service will sometimes buy a company to gain access to a complimentary product that can be sold to its existing customer base. We currently have a client who makes and distributes baked goods to restaurants. He is looking to purchase a company that makes other types of desserts or related items to add to his current baked goods line.

- **Preferred Locations (Retail)**

For a retail business or restaurant, location is a key ingredient for success. For this reason, retailers will buy companies with the goal of buying a favorable location. An enhancement in this type of acquisition is a location that is already set up for the kind of business that the acquirer wants to place there.

As mentioned in Chapter IV, a successful sandwich shop chain gave us a list of neighborhoods and said they would be interested in purchasing a small restaurant in any of the neighborhoods. They were buying desirable locations and in-place equipment. They converted each location to their own name and menu. It was cheaper to do this than to rent a space and buy and install equipment.

- **Favorable Lease**

Occasionally a company will have a long term lease at below market rates. For example, a retailer may have signed a lease in a less than perfect location. However, the area may have changed for the better due to gentrification, changing traffic patterns, or other evolutionary developments. If you can buy a retail business that has a 15 year lease at, $5.00 per square foot, while the other stores in the area are paying $15.00 per square foot, you have the makings of a great business advantage. The lease could only be transferred to you if there were a lease provision stating that it were transferrable, or if the holder of the lease were a corporation, and the business were sold on a stock sale basis (see Chapter XIII).

- **Trade Name or Trade Mark**

Also as discussed in Chapter IV a trusted product or company name can be an asset worth buying. If a company that manufactures industrial electrical items wanted to expand and offer batteries in consumer markets, it would almost certainly do better if it had a recognizable name to use like *GE*, or *Eveready*. Consumers would be far more likely to choose a familiar brand name. This would be true even if the exact same batteries were offered under a different brand name. That is, the consumer faced with a choice of a name brand battery and an unknown battery is far more likely to choose the brand name product.

The same is true of a retail store. A store with a known name will in all likelihood sell more than a similar store without a recognized and established name.

- **Elimination of Competitors**

There are acquisitions carried out with the primary goal of eliminating a competitor. Recall the example from Chapter IV about a convenience store that was bought by the convenience store up the street. The acquiring company was than able to raise prices without worry about being undersold by its former competitor. While this example is a bit extreme, it is not uncommon for a buyer to buy a competitor merely to create a less competitive marketplace.

Acquiring is Lower Risk

Generally speaking, purchasing a company is inherently less risky than are most other newly implemented expansion efforts. A marketing practice that has been in place for years and worked well is, of course, the least risky expansion option. Any new marketing effort, however, is an iffy proposition, especially if the goal is to create quick and dramatic results.

Before acquiring a company you will have access to financial records, in place practices that have been honed over the years, and often times an established base of repeat customers. This is clearly an advantage over untried marketing and sales efforts.

We advise clients to evaluate a prospective acquisition by comparing it to the alternatives in terms of cost, likelihood of success, and time. That is, what would it cost, for example, to gain 100 new customers versus what would it cost to buy a company with 100 customers that are easily transferrable? Also, factor in the likelihood of attaining the goal of gaining and keeping customers through either method. Finally, consider how long it would take to achieve the goal. While buying is decidedly quicker once a prospective target company is available, finding a target company can be a time consuming process.

More Financing Options

While most growth strategies must be financed through internal funding or venture capital, lenders will often look favorably upon funding an acquisition. Bankers don't respond well to new or untried plans no matter how well they may be presented. They are trained to rely on financial statements and plans that place realistic reliance on those statements. When acquiring a company, such information can be furnished giving the banker something to analyze and to base a decision upon.

- **Seller Financing**

Finally, the magic that makes many acquisitions possible is seller financing. A seller will often agree to finance some percentage of an acquisition. Further, the seller will usually agree to take a position subordinate to a bank so seller financing will not interfere with bank financing. Typically, the seller will be secured by the business being conveyed, and nothing more. If you purchase a company, and default on paying for it, the old owner will take back the business. While the going business as security will not impress a banker or other traditional lender, that going business will have security value to the seller who presumably has the capability to run it. Financing is discussed in more detail in Chapter XI.

Planning the Acquisition

As with all business ventures, careful planning is a key to success. A well executed acquisition typically includes a good business plan. The only problem here is that a full business plan cannot be prepared until an appropriate acquisition target is found. Obviously, the nature and direction of the target company will impact the business plan.

Before getting to the point of a specific target company and a business plan, a few preliminary steps are in order.

- **Acquisition Goals**

    The first step is to clearly define exactly what you want the acquisition to accomplish. Typical acquisition goals include:

    - expansion
    - elimination of competition
    - economies of scale (utilization of excess capacities)
    - new products
    - new distribution channels
    - larger customer base

These possibilities were discussed above and in Chapter IV.

Writing down your goals will help immeasurably. The time it takes to commit it to writing will save hours of looking at and analyzing businesses that are inappropriate for acquisition.

- **Acquisition Summary**

    We recommend that you prepare an *acquisition summary* ;which will incorporate the acquisition goals. The summary will contain additional information such as:

    - overview of the buying company
    - a somewhat detailed description of the type of acquisition sought
    - geographical requirements
    - size requirements (in volume, number of employees, or other quantifiable criteria)

- preferred timetable for making an acquisition
- profitability requirements
- management requirements
- outline of your plan to finance the acquisition
- anything that would make a prospective acquisition company unacceptable to you

This summary will be used for at least two purposes. First, it will help you to clarify your own reasons for pursuing an acquisition and the benefits that you will gain from that acquisition. Organizing your thoughts and committing them to paper is an essential step toward a realistic evaluation of your plans. You may well find that some of your vague ideas and thoughts either coalesce or fall apart when you are called upon to put them into a well organized written plan. If they coalesce, great — go forward. If they fall apart, you have spent a few hours to save many more hours of time and many dollars of dubious investment capital.

Second, the acquisition summary will serve as a clear communication tool to both intermediaries and prospective acquisition targets. Lawyers, accountants, business brokers and other intermediaries may be in a position to help you find a suitable company. However, if you merely tell them verbally what you are looking for, it will have far less impact than a clear and concise written document. Further, a written summary will demonstrate your seriousness in pursuing this objective.

We get calls all the time from people interested in buying companies. On occasion, we get a written summary that clearly spells out what a prospective buyer is looking for. The verbal request is entered into a computer database with a brief description. However, the written summary is studied carefully and has a much better chance of being acted upon. Right or wrong, we assume that the person (or company) who provided the written request, even if it is only a page or two long, is a far better prospect because of the effort that went into its preparation.

Evaluating Feasibility

Some types of companies are quite easy to find and buy, while others are extremely difficult. Further, the level of difficulty of finding different types of companies is changing all the time depending on the local and regional economy, political changes, and other changes. In southern New England right now, for example, retail stores and restaurants for sale are very easy to find, while finding quality manufacturing firms is difficult.

Discovering the general availability of the kind of business you are interested in acquiring is a relatively easy matter. You can try some of the following steps:

- **Business Brokers** — Call around to several business brokers; in the area where you are seeking an acquisition. Spell out your acquisition criteria clearly and ask what may be available. If there is nothing, ask how likely it is that something will be available of that type within the next few months. Ask, "How often do you handle this type of business? How many have you handled in the last year?" Your goal is not necessarily to find out what is now available, but to find out how often the type of firm you want becomes available.

Some business brokers specialize in a certain size of company and type of industry(s). Don't, for example, put too much stock in what a broker who specializes in retail stores selling for under $80,000 tells you about availability of financial service firms grossing over $2,000,000. Business brokers are discussed in more detail in Chapter VI.

- **Newspapers** — Most major local newspapers carry a classified ad section that advertises businesses for sale. The section is generally titled *Business Opportunities* or something similar. Checking this section, particularly on Sundays, will give you an overview of what is available.

Many local papers tend to carry a lot of advertising for smaller less sophisticated companies. If you are looking for a larger firm, checking a paper from a larger city in your region may be a good idea. Right or wrong, sellers with more substantial operations often assume that the people or organizations with the financial resources to make larger investments read big city papers.

Finally, some more substantial businesses choose the *Wall Street Journal* as the medium to announce a business sale. *The Mart*, the section in that paper that advertises businesses for sale is certainly worth a check. A warning here is that the *Wall Street Journal* publishes a number of regional editions. Advertisers of businesses for sale will often advertise only in the region where they are located. For this reason, you must buy the appropriate geographic edition to get a good idea of what is available in your target location.

- **Trade Press** — Local, regional, and national industry-specific publications also have sections advertising businesses for sale. Check in the appropriate industry publications and in those of related industries.

- **Supplier Representatives** — As you know, industrial salespeople can often be great sources of information. It couldn't hurt to ask them how often they hear of businesses for sale in your industry.

For more detailed information on various avenues to explore for finding an appropriate acquisition, or for examining the feasibility of a planned acquisition, see Chapter V (Finding A Business To Buy).

Company to Company Versus Individual Acquisitions

A company buying a business typically has a different set of evaluation criteria than does an individual or group buying a firm. A company is looking for synergies — areas where the two companies can work together to ultimately be more than the sum of their parts. While profitability of the target company is certainly a consideration, it is only one of the important factors. If, for example, a company is breaking even, but an acquiring company can maintain sales and margins of that company while eliminating $100,000 of its overhead, that company can in essence be earning $100,000 for the acquiring company.

A buyer that is not buying a company to take advantage of company to company synergies must look at an acquisition opportunity differently. Such a buyer is typically looking for a *turnkey* opportunity. That is, the proposed acquisition must make financial sense based upon its current financial performance. Such a buyer does not have aces up his sleeve such as the ability to immediately take a new product to existing channels, reduce overhead, or take advantage of existing but underutilized production equipment.

For the most part, small businesses are offered, bought, and sold on a turnkey basis. Businesses that make sense based on their profitability to price ratio are not that difficult to sell. It is merely a matter of convincing a buyer that the investment will result in a good rate of return compared to other investments on a risk versus return basis.

However, there are many businesses available that have little value as stand alone investments, but may have a great deal of value to a buyer who can take synergistic advantage of them. These businesses can provide excellent opportunities for the right buyer. If you can find such a business, that would work synergistically with your company, you may well be able to consummate a win-win deal whereby you buy a business at a fraction of what it is worth to you, while the seller receives more than any turnkey buyer would consider paying. One man's junk can truly be another man's (or in this case another company's) treasure. It is this kind of situation that an acquiring company should be on the lookout for.

X Preparing a Business Plan

A business plan is like a road map, tailored for a specific journey. It details where you are starting from, where you are going, and most importantly the route you will take to get there.

Most of us recognize the usefulness of a road map for a long trip. However, many of us do not understand the usefulness of a business plan for the far more complex venture of buying and growing a business. A business plan is important to any business, especially one that is about to be taken over and run by a new manager(s). Even if you as the buyer do not agree with the need for a plan, in all likelihood you will have to prepare at least a rudimentary plan for a lender, investor, or virtually any source of outside financing.

The act of preparing a written business plan will help you to clarify and improve your own thoughts on a business direction. In some cases, putting it on paper can help you to realize that the planned endeavor is not as promising as first thought. This is an unfortunate realization, but better it should come at this stage than after you have invested countless hours and thousands of dollars. On the other hand, writing a plan can help you to recognize and define opportunities that were less visible when they were merely *floating around in your head.*

Business Plan Versus Business Description

Our opinion is no different than that of most other business advisors. A business plan is essential to a business. However, our opinion does differ in one aspect. Many lenders, especially when dealing with smaller companies on loans that are fully secured by collateral, ask for business plans, but really want only business descriptions. The only real difference between the two is the amount of detail required and the amount of emphasis placed on future business improvements or changes.

For venture financing or substantial debt financing you will need a full fledged business plan. To enhance your own prospects of making your business succeed, a full business plan may well be worth the effort. Nevertheless, a briefer business summary may suffice for certain business loan situations.

A lender who is backed 100% by collateral really is concerned with gaining only a basic understanding of the business. In fact, bankers by nature are skeptical of major changes in the way a company is run. They would often prefer to see a summary that explains how a business is being run, how finances work (how money is earned), and above all else, how cash flow will adequately service the requested debt.

Current and past (at least three years) financial statements are at the heart of a plan (or summary) for an acquisition. Projected financial statements are next in importance. Typically, lenders like to see three to five years of projected statements. Everyone understands that projections are to a degree based on assumptions. However, they should be as well documented and defended as possible. Merely to say you anticipate sales growth of 30% per year is not adequate. If your sales growth projections, though, are based on clear steps or occurrences such as beefing up a sales force, documented market expansion, or clear market growth trends in the projected range, the projections will be more credible.

The Appendix contains an outline that can be followed in developing a brief business plan or business summary. This outline, while easier than most to follow, will help you prepare a basic business plan suitable for a variety of applications. If you need a more detailed plan, there are a number of books on the subject listed in the Appendix.

XI Financing a Deal

There are several methods of financing a business buyout. Most of the basic methods have a myriad of variations available. The methods outlined below are some of the more common approaches. However they are often used in combination with different kinds of modifications and twists. As with most other transactions in a market based economy, buyer and seller are free to negotiate any terms and any prices that they wish.

Seller Financing (Taking Paper)

Most buyers would prefer to get nearly 100% of a deal financed by the seller. Most sellers would prefer the opposite- to get 100% cash for their business. Most transactions happen somewhere in between those two extremes. The fact is, however, that seller financing or *taking back paper* is the magic that makes many small business acquisitions happen.

Any small business owner will testify to the difficulties involved in borrowing from a bank. The bank nearly always wants collateral in the form of real estate or something else of tangible value. Seldom is the business alone enough to secure financing. From the banker's point of view this makes sense. If the business owner can't pay a loan, real estate (your house!) can be easily sold. Business equipment and failing businesses are a different story, though. From a banker's perspective, a business and its assets have value only as long as they are earning money. The last thing a banker wants to do is come in and take over a small business that he knows nothing about running.

However, a business owner presumably does know how to run his business. If you buy a business and can't meet the payments on the seller's loan, then the seller can take the business back and run it. The security in the business (that the seller will insist upon holding) has real value to that seller but has only minimal value to the bank. Further the seller usually will get a reasonably good rate on the money he is lending. While rates on seller financing vary, a rate of prime or a bit higher is typical. That is, most owner financed deals are financed at a rate lower than a bank will charge on a small business loan, but higher than it will pay on a CD or savings account.

The argument to make to a seller is, "If you finance the deal (under the parameters outlined, above), you have a secured loan at a rate of interest higher than a bank will pay you for your money." You can enhance the attractiveness of the offer by guaranteeing the note personally which adds a measure of assurance that the seller will be paid. However, we would guarantee personally only if there were no other alternatives short of pulling out of the deal.

In practice, most business sales include some owner financing, typically 20% to 50% of the total, but sometimes higher. If the security is strong (tangible assets, real property, personal guarantees, or specific assets as outlined below) then a higher amount of owner financing is reasonable to request.

Price and terms go hand in hand. A lower purchase price may not be as good as a higher price with better terms. While a price is easy to compare with another price as better or worse, terms are much more difficult to evaluate and compare. An owner who needs cash immediately to cover his son's tuition bill will not view payment over 5 years as positively as someone who is less pressed for immediate cash.

Seller financing then:

- can be your easiest, and in some instances your only source of financing
- earns the seller a decent rate of return on a low risk investment
- can make a deal happen, that otherwise would fail

Bank Financing

Most buyers turn to banks for some part of the financing to buy a business. Banks lend money only if they can be convinced that the risk of not getting repaid is minimal. As of this writing, bank lending for small business is exceptionally tight. Even in the best of economic times, banks need to be convinced that:

a) the cash flow of the business is adequate to service (repay as scheduled) the loan, and

b) even if the business can't make timely payments from cash flow, the bank has security in the form of collateral that can be converted to cash so the bank can get repaid.

Item b) means simply that the bank will insist that the borrower have something of value that can be taken away from him or her if the loan can not be repaid as planned. Typically, this means the buyer's house or other real estate, stocks or bonds, or other items of clear value that can be converted to cash with relative ease.

It is a widely held misconception among buyers that banks will lend money to a small business and accept the assets of the business as the only collateral. While the bank will generally insist on the assets of the business as collateral, most of these assets will be *discounted* dramatically. Only rarely can a small business loan be secured only by the assets of the business.

For example, suppose that you want to purchase a business for $150,000. The business has approximately $60,000 in inventory (at cost), and about $40,000 worth of production equipment at fair market value. You reason that the bank will lend up to $100,000 based on the inventory and equipment as collateral.

In reality, the bank will reason that the inventory can be sold or otherwise *disappear* before they can take it if the loan falls behind. Further, despite the value of $60,000, the banker does not have the facilities, expertise, or desire to sell the inventory. As far as the equipment, which may have $40,000 of value to you or anyone using it to manufacture a product, to the banker it has far less value. He is not going to manufacture anything with it. Worse, he reasons, "The last thing I want to do is have to pay to store the stuff, and get involved in auctioning it off." If your banker is like most, he doesn't even want to see it, let alone sell it.

If you're lucky, the bank will lend you $20,000 based on the assets that are genuinely worth $100,000 to you. The rest of the collateral will have to come from other sources such as personal guarantees secured by real estate or other hard assets that can be converted quickly to cash.

Finally, it is important to point out that a bank will insist on *being in first position* for any collateral. This means that any other lender will not receive collateral or money that comes from the collateral until the bank is paid in full. The implications in a buy/sell deal are that if the seller is providing financing with the business as collateral, he or she is taking a bigger risk than the bank because the bank gets paid all they are owed, before the other lenders get anything.

Enhanced Seller Financing

While the bank will be cool to accepting inventory and business equipment as security, you may be able to squeeze some more borrowing power from it through another route. As previously discussed, seller financing is a favorable method of financing an acquisition. A twist to seller financing involves specific assets as security for the seller.

The inventory has very limited value to the bank, at best 20% of its value at cost. However, the seller who knows what to do with the inventory may be convinced to accept it as security for a much higher proportion of its value, perhaps 75% or even 100%. Under such a scenario, the seller would hold a note secured by the inventory. In all likelihood you as the buyer would have to agree not to let inventory fall below a specified level based upon the amount of money owed against it.

The seller, not the bank, would be in first position, but only for the inventory. This, of course, will reduce the amount the bank will lend (a loan backed only by a second position on inventory is all but worthless to a bank), but the amount of the loss will be more than made up for by the increased seller financing.

The same type of arrangement can be made for business equipment, and even for accounts receivable. If the seller will accept an asset as collateral at a higher value than a bank, you are that much closer to achieving the needed financing.

Small Business Administration (SBA)

There are a number of misconceptions regarding loans from the Small Business Administration. The vast majority of SBA activity in small business lending isn't really lending at all. Rather, it involves guaranteeing bank loans. If the borrower can not repay the loan, the U.S. government will repay most of it to the bank. Typically, the SBA will guarantee up to 85% or 90% of the loan amount. This means that the bank can charge interest on the full amount of the loan, but it will be at risk for as little as 10% of that loan. An SBA guarantee is a useful vehicle to consider for a loan that is marginal. A loan for $100,000 secured by $300,000 in real estate (equity value) requested by a small business manager with a good track record, will not need the SBA. Finding a bank to do that kind of deal should not be difficult. On the other hand, a request for $100,000 with no security, made by a prospective buyer with no management experience, will be turned down by virtually all banks, and by the SBA. The situations in the middle that are almost but not quite low risk enough for traditional bank borrowing are the best candidates for SBA guarantees.

Commercial bankers regularly deal with the SBA and should be familiar with its loan requirements. If a loan is turned down, talk with the banker about the possibility of an SBA guarantee. You can go to the SBA yourself, but going through the banker will probably prove a more efficient route.

An SBA guarantee involves a lot of paper work. Like a traditional bank loan, it also usually involves collateral. However, he SBA does tend to be a bit looser on collateral requirements. Also the SBA will generally allow longer payback periods than a bank will, so monthly loan payments can be lower.

- **SBA Direct Programs**

  There is much talk about direct SBA loans for women, minorities, veterans, and handicapped persons. Unfortunately it is mostly just that — talk. While several SBA direct programs do exist, they are sporadically funded. It is a bit like someone keeping 10 bank accounts but with no significant funds in any one account. While the accounts would indeed exist, they would not be worth a whole lot.

  In the past three years, the only SBA direct loans that we have seen were a handful of loans granted through the SBA Vietnam era veteran's program. The funds available vary from office to office. If you served in the armed forces during the Vietnam era, and are interested in applying for a direct loan under this program, ask your local SBA office for information.

Leveraged Buyout

A leveraged buyout is simply a buyout financed in part by a bank or another financial institution. The assets of the business are used as collateral for borrowing.

While many if not most small businesses are bought with bank financing, the assets of the business are of limited value as collateral, as explained above. The bank will generally insist that more *solid* assets (such as real estate) be pledged before they will finance a small business deal.

State and Municipal Lending Programs

Some states and some cities maintain business lending programs. Such programs can be either loan guarantee programs or direct lending, or a combination of both. A good place to find out what programs may be available would be your state or city economic development office or your local chamber of commerce. Such sources are long shots, but we have seen a number of deals made possible by public or quasi-public business lending programs.

Venture Capital

Venture capital is money invested in a company, as opposed to money lent to a company. A venture capitalist typically makes a relatively large investment in a company with significant growth potential. Unlike a traditional investment in a public company's stock, a venture investment usually entails the investor(s)'s gaining a significant proportion of a firm's corporate stock, as well as a significant voice as to how the investment money is used. In practical terms, venture capital is usually invested based upon a specific and detailed plan proposed by management of the company.

Seldom will a venture capitalist insist on a controlling interest in a firm, but 35% to 40% equity ownership is not uncommon. Because venture capitalists invest in less established and higher risk ventures, they expect a correspondingly higher return on their investment.

While an investor in AT&T, for example, may be delighted with a 10% to 12% annual return, a venture capitalist often expects a return of 25% to 35% due to the higher risk involved. It is the job of company management to convince a venture capitalist (or venture capital company) that attaining such an ambitious goal is not only possible but likely. Given that venture capitalists are accustomed to starry eyed entrepreneurs, and the contrasting realities of risky ventures, convincing a venture investor that yours is the exceptional company that will deliver a very high return is no easy task.

While venture capital is popularly associated with startup situations, many venture capitalists prefer acquisitions. They understand that acquiring a company is generally less risky than starting one, and that past performance can be used as a basis for predicting future performance.

Whether starting a business or acquiring one, the first thing that you will need is a good .i.business plan;. A venture capitalist will expect a detailed plan and will analyze it thoroughly before considering an investment.

Business Plans are discussed in more detail in Chapter X.

- **Small Business Investment Companies (SBIC)**

  A SBIC is a venture capital company that is partly financed by the Small Business Administration. SBICs are generally administered by banks and other financial institutions. While they have government and bank involvement, they are venture capital companies in all respects. Call your local SBA office or some of the larger banks in your area to find out about local SBICs.

- **Angels**

   An angel is a sort of part-time or informal venture capitalist. A typical angel is a person who has made a good deal of money, probably in a business venture, who likes to get involved in promising startups or acquisitions. Angels often have valuable experience and knowledge as well as money to bring to the venture.

   The only problem with angels is that they are extremely difficult to find. You would not, for example, have much luck going to the yellow pages and looking under "Angels." Private venture investors do not want the publicity and the inconvenience that often comes with the community's knowing that they invest in young companies. Generally, they must find you, or you must be referred to them through lawyers, accountants, brokers, or business associates.

   Another possible channel to find interested angels is an organization called *The Venture Capital Network*. This organization puts angels together with business plans submitted by companies looking for investment capital. The angels receive a business plan(s), and if they are interested will contact the company. You can contact VCN at: Venture Capital Network, Inc., PO Box 882, Durham, NH 03824, (603) 743-3993.

Silent Partners

While the label "silent partner" is used for a variety of partnership situations, here we use it to mean a type of investor who wants to acquire a company but in association with another individual(s) who will take day to day management responsibility. This situation is similar to an investment by an angel, except the silent partner will often demand a controlling interest in the venture. If you know a wealthy individual who wants to buy a business but doesn't want to work full time running it, a proposal to that person may be worth your while.

Earn Outs

An earn out is an arrangement whereby part of the seller's compensation for the business is based on the performance of the business after the deal is closed. For example, let's suppose that a seller is asking $200,000 for his business which includes $80,000 of inventory at cost, and $20,000 of equipment and other tangible assets at fair market value. A buyer may offer $100,000 at closing with an additional payment of 20% of the firm's gross sales over the twelve months following closing.

Rather than gross sales, the benchmark can be net sales or net profits (as long as net profits are clearly defined). The point is that the seller's compensation is tied to the performance of the business in some way.

Earn outs are often used when buyer and seller disagree as to the projected performance of the business or in a situation where poor records make an analysis of past performance difficult.

Earn outs are also typical if there exists the possibility of an extraordinary event that will significantly impact the business's performance, either positively or negatively. For example, suppose you want to buy a certain doughnut shop, but there is a proposal for a major competitor to open up a block away. This will likely cause you concern and justifiably so. However, an earn out structure might make the deal more acceptable because the seller and you will then essentially be sharing the risk of the unwanted proposal's being accepted.

Similarly, suppose you want to buy a manufacturing firm, but the owner is hesitant to sell because a major contract is on the verge of coming through. Under an earn out agreement, if it does come through, the seller will receive some of the financial benefit whereas if it doesn't come through, you will not be paying for a contract that never materializes.

Consulting and Employment Fees

It is not unusual to pay an agreed amount for a business plus a guaranteed salary or consulting fee to the seller for a negotiated period of time. Sometimes a seller will be paid an inflated salary or consulting fee with the understanding that the inflated amount is actually compensation for the business. The effect here is to assure the seller's continual help and cooperation in running the business. A warning here is to talk with your accountants before entering into a clearly inflated compensation agreement. Such an agreement has tax advantages to you but may be challenged by the IRS. This issue is discussed more fully in Chapter XIV.

Keep it Simple

It has been our experience that the more complex the deal is, the more likely it is to fall through. Some people, advisors and principals alike, love the challenge of structuring deals with options, separate corporations, graduated earn out provisions, and a host of other elements. Sometimes these complexities are necessary tools to bringing a deal to fruition. More often in small business transactions, such complexities lead to misunderstandings between buyer and seller. At best these misunderstandings require highly paid advisors to untangle and explain, and at worst lead to someone backing out of the deal because they don't understand it.

We recently had this happen to us. A buyer proposed a relatively complex deal. The buyer indicated that he didn't understand it. He asked us to explain it to his lawyer and his CPA, which we did. Both his lawyer and CPA told him the deal looked good. He went along with the deal but later indicated that an important element was different than he thought it was. He then decided that he would not go along with this deal, or any deal that he couldn't understand himself. We were back to square one.

Chapter Summary

Buyer and seller are free to construct a deal in virtually any way they wish. While the basic methods are described above, any combination or any other methods that buyer and seller come up with are fair game. It is not unusual for a creative financing structure to resurrect a dead deal or to make an unattractive business much more attractive. However, you are advised to keep the deal from getting any more complex than is necessary. The more complex the deal, the more likely it is to fall through.

XII Negotiating the Deal

Negotiating to buy a business is not different than other kinds of negotiations. There are books, courses, and programs available on negotiating techniques that can help you if you feel you need help.

This section will cover some of the important elements of the process specifically as they relate to acquiring a business.

Think Like the Seller

Before entering into a buy/sell negotiation, try to put yourself in the seller's position. While you may think that the asking price is far from reasonable, consider how the seller feels. He may intellectually understand that you are not concerned about the work of the past, but rather about the future potential. However, this business represents years of labor and risk. Emotionally, selling the business represents at least the closing of a chapter of his life. The deal that is finally consummated determines the sweetness or bitterness of the close of that chapter. The more you can appreciate where the seller is coming from, the better you will be able to handle the negotiating process.

Be Polite and Respectful from the Start

Business owners are very sensitive about their businesses. The worst thing you can do is to give the seller the message that you think he mismanaged the business and that you can easily improve the operation. It is far more productive to compliment the seller where you can, and keep your negative observations to yourself. Surprisingly, good feelings about a prospective buyer can be incredibly important to a deal's success. On the other hand, buyer insensitivity to an owner can destroy a deal before it has had a chance to develop.

Do not Insult the Seller with a Low Ball Offer

Some amateur negotiators reason that the lower the original offer the better. After all, the reasoning continues, "I can always increase the offer." However, the sale of a business is too emotional for the seller for that strategy to work well. If your offer is too far from an acceptable range, he or she may walk away and refuse to even talk about it any more. We have seen more than one seller get so insulted by a low offer that just out of spite they sold their businesses to someone else for less than the insulting prospective buyers eventually offered.
It is a good idea to discuss, or at least hint at, the price range you will offer before actually making an offer. By doing so, the seller will at least have a general understanding of what to expect. As a rule of thumb offer no more than fifteen percent lower than you are prepared to pay. Often it is better strategy to negotiate on terms rather than on price where possible (see *Impasse Busting* below).

Every Seller has other Deals Pending

It is a common strategy for sellers to tell buyers that they have other deals on the floor. They, of course, do this to pressure you, to extract concessions, and to get you to move faster. By the same token, prospective buyers like to tell sellers about the many businesses that they currently have under consideration.

Sometimes it's true; sometimes it's not true, and most times it's somewhere in between. That is, a seller may be quick to point out how he received three offers but not so quick to point out that none of them was even in the ball park of acceptability. A buyer may be quick to talk about the six firms he's looking at, but he is not so quick to explain that three are out of his price range, and two don't interest him.

Our advice in general is to brush off talk of other prospects. You don't know how true it may be, and even if you did there is very little that you can do to control what happens with other deals. However, delay will only enhance the possibility that another deal will become a threat to you.

Keep Emotions out of Negotiations

It is advisable to use an intermediary in the negotiating process to assure that emotions don't get in the way of striking the best deal possible. An intermediary such as a business broker (not the same one who is already part of the deal as the seller's agent) or a lawyer, will be less emotionally invested in the process and better able to negotiate effectively.

Look for Win-Win Negotiation

The old school of negotiating was that every negotiation had a winner and loser, defined by who got the best deal. The new school is that both sides can come up winners; there does not have to be a loser. Both the buyer and seller can get what they want without *defeating* the other party. You may be prepared to pay $200,000 for a business. That may be a great price if, for example, it would cost far more than that to start your own company and develop it to the point of profitability that the seller has already attained. It may also be a great deal for the seller if he started it on $20,000, he's ready to retire, and he has calculated that as long as he gets over $150,000 for the business, his retirement is financially secure.

Striving for a win-win negotiation lessens the chance of destructive friction and of a full breakdown of negotiations. Of course you won't agree on every point. But you can think in terms of looking for ways to make all parties involved feel that they are getting most of what they want.

Impasse Busting — Negotiate Terms

Sometimes sellers will decide on a price and refuse to sell for a dollar less. If you run into this situation, keep in mind that it is human nature to avoid going back on one's resolution. Instead of negotiating on price, concentrate on terms. For example, "I'll consider paying your price, but let's talk about payment terms. Can you consider financing 35% of the deal at 3% below prime?" A scenario like this, if accepted, means that the seller does not have to back down, and the buyer gets the net effect of a lower price anyway.

You can also try to use non-cash *sweeteners* in lieu of a higher price. Some non-cash *sweeteners* include:

- Providing free or cheap use of office space for the seller after the sale.
- Secretarial and related assistance on an occasional basis.
- Discounts on the company's products or services for the seller's family.
- Allowing the seller to keep assets that you don't need (copy machines, fax machines, coffee makers, computers, etc.).
- Part time employment for the seller's children.
- Increasing the security on seller financing.

Don't Get Bogged down on Small Points

Both of us have, on more than one occasion, been involved in negotiations that would look downright silly to an outsider. There have been situations where buyer and seller have come to terms on six figure sell prices but argue about who gets the next twelve issues of a magazine whose subscription fee was paid for two months previously. Recently at a closing for a business selling for $110,000 buyer and seller spent 15 minutes debating about $200 worth of stationery. Perhaps arguing the small points relieves the tensions of the negotiation. That's fine. However, be careful not to let a very small point wreck the whole deal or distract attention from substantive issues.

During negotiating sessions, we have often suggested dropping a point and coming back to it later if we feel it is relatively insignificant, and it is bogging down discussions. When we do this, half the time the buyer and seller forget all about the point that was causing such bitter debate until we bring it up or decide to let it be forgotten forever.

Blame Lawyers, Brokers, Brothers, Advisors, Accountants

A common but effective ploy used in negotiating the sale of a business is to blame another person as the bad guy. It's used like this, "I'd agree to pay your price but my accountant just won't let me do it." Or, "Gee you know I trust your inventory count, but the bank insists that we do a physical count on closing day."

You can always be the good guy while one of your advisors or associates is making all the tough demands. This strategy is especially useful if you will continue to work with the former owner, and you need his or her continued cooperation. The advisor can be the whipping boy while the principals to the deal preserve their friendly relationship.

Chapter Summary

A buy/sell transaction often involves an emotionally charged negotiation. While emotions can be expected to run high, it is best to keep discussions as business-like as possible. Intermediaries may help achieve this. Sometimes impasses can be broken by negotiating terms rather than price, and by offering non-cash sweeteners. Finally, your goal should be a win-win, not a win-lose negotiation.

XIII   Legal Issues

It is essential that you consult an attorney before buying a business. However, it is generally not necessary to bring your lawyer into the picture until you are ready to make an offer. Most of what a lawyer has to contribute comes later in the process — once an offer is made. Under all circumstances, do talk to your lawyer before you sign any commitment to purchase a company.

Some of the legal issues involved in buying a company are outlined below:

Stock Versus Asset Sale

---

* **Stock Sale**

   One way that you can buy a corporation is through the purchase of shares of its stock. In this scenario, you would keep the corporate structure of the acquired company. The stock that the owners of the selling company own would be sold to you for the agreed upon price and terms. The legally created entity of the corporation would continue under the new owner. As the new owner, you would probably replace the officers and directors of the corporation.

   A purchase by corporate stock is often the vehicle of choice if there is to be a partial buyout. If you wanted, for example, to buy into a corporation at 25%, 50%, 60% or any other proportion, you would merely buy that percentage of stock in the corporation. Compared to the alternatives, a stock sale makes partial ownership transition relatively simple.

   One interesting advantage of a sale by corporate stock is that leases and other agreements made by the corporation would remain intact unless there were specific lease provisions dealing with changes in ownership. If, for example, the corporation had a lease with very favorable terms, that lease could be passed on to the new owner without the landlord's specific permission.

   There are businesses bought where a favorable lease is the target firm's most valuable asset. For example, a retailer may have a long term lease with extremely favorable rates relative to current market rates. A buyer might take over the company (on a stock purchase basis) primarily to take advantage of the existing lease.

   A second interesting advantage of a sale by corporate stock is that tax credits and or tax loss carry forwards on the tax return of the corporation, pass along to the new owner. This in and of itself may have value to some buyers. Consult your accountant to determine if a loss carry forward might be useful to you.

   From the seller's point of view, an advantage of a sale by corporate stock is that it could save on taxes. Under an asset sale, a C-corporation's owner(s) might be taxed twice- first on the corporate level, then on the individual level.

If you were to buy a company on a stock sale basis , unless it were specifically stated otherwise, all cash, accounts receivables, property, and other assets would, upon closing, belong to you. All liabilities such as accounts payable, short term debt, and long term debt would also become your responsibility. However, if any loans are guaranteed personally by the seller (or by anyone), the personal guarantee(s) would stay intact unless specific arrangements were made with the lender.

A problem to watch out for in a purchase by corporate stock is that any legal action brought against the corporation for past events, or any tax liabilities including those from previous years, would be your responsibility, unless the seller were to specifically agree otherwise. Even in the case of specific agreements for past liabilities or legal action for past occurrences, you as the new owner would have to contend with the situation and then collect from the previous owner. Potential liabilities unknown to the seller at the time of sale are also inherited by the buyer. One classic example is the liability for asbestos related injuries.

If the IRS were to audit a corporation after it were sold but for a period that it was owned by the previous owner, it could hold the corporation (meaning its new owner) responsible. The new owner would have to cooperate with the audit, and if past taxes were due, the corporation would be responsible, so far as the IRS is concerned.

Because of the potential liabilities of *skeletons in the closet*, it is important to exercise great care in buying corporations through the sale of stock. If you do buy a corporation in this way, insist that the seller take responsibility for any and all previous liabilities, and that he guarantee, through sworn statement, the assets and liabilities and general accuracy and completeness of the balance sheet.

- **Asset Sale**

Another way to buy a company is on an asset sale basis. In an asset sale, you would buy some or all of the firm's tangible and intangible assets such as equipment, patents, customer lists, business name, and goodwill; shares of stock do not change hands. The existing corporation essentially sells off the assets to the buyer which can be an individual, partnership, or corporation. To add a layer of protection against possible liability, lawyers often advise buyers to set up a corporation to buy the assets.

Often in an asset sale, cash, accounts receivables, and all liabilities would remain with the previous owner's corporation. The company would be delivered free of debt to the new owner. The accounts receivable would be paid to the old corporation, and therefore to the seller. Some people feel that it is important to buy the receivables as part of the transaction. The logic here is that:

a) it gives you more control over the customer list which is often the major asset being purchased.

b) it can prevent bookkeeping problems and disagreements, such as allocating partial payments, credits, returns, etc.

Unlike with a purchase via corporate stock, leases and other agreements are not automatically transferred. Unless the lease agreement specifically stated that it were assignable, a new lease would have to be negotiated with the landlord.

In the case of a partial buyout, an asset sale is a bit more cumbersome, but still workable. If you were planning a partial buyout on a stock sale basis, you would purchase the agreed upon proportion of the firm's corporate stock. In an asset sale, you would likely set up a new corporation to buy the assets of the selling corporation. Stock in the new corporation would be divided between buyer and seller based upon the agreed proportion of ownership.

It is best to buy closely held corporations on an asset sale basis if it can be done without damaging the value of the company being bought. The primary reason for this is the problem of taking on unexpected liabilities. However, in some situations a stock sale is the only way to achieve your buying objective. For example, if the main reason for buying a company is that it holds a favorable lease that is not otherwise transferrable, a stock sale is the only good option.

Buying Unincorporated Companies

In essence, an unincorporated company must either be purchased on an asset basis, or it must first be incorporated, and then sold on a corporate stock basis. However, there is no reason that an existing or a newly formed corporation can not purchase a proprietorship. This is often done to facilitate a partial acquisition of an unincorporated firm.

A partial sale under this scenario would be achieved as follows: A corporation is formed by buyer and seller. Stock is divided between buyer and seller based upon the agreed ownership proportions. Then, the new corporation purchases the seller's unincorporated firm. The result: each party now owns the agreed proportion of the acquired company, as it is absorbed into the new corporation.

Bulk Sales Act

All 50 states of the United States have agreed to a set of rules and regulations known as the **Uniform Commercial Code** (UCC). In short the UCC is a body of laws and regulations that govern commercial transactions.

One provision of the UCC commonly referred to as "The Bulk Sales Act", is relevant to the sale of businesses. The Bulk Sales Act essentially protects the creditors of a business from the possible sale in bulk of the assets of that business for the purpose of defrauding those creditors. That is, a business owner can not sell off his business or major parts thereof without creditors being notified of his intention, and having the opportunity to legally object to the sale.

The application of the bulk sales provisions vary from state to state, but the intent and effect is the same. Creditors must be notified before the sale closes. If they are not, the option exists for them to overturn the sale, and/or to collect from the buyer (or seller or both). In some states it is the seller's responsibility, and in other states, the seller must notify the buyer, and the buyer has the responsibility of notifying the creditors. The notification, in some states, must be given thirty days before the close. A creditor who intends to act, must do so during the prescribed period.

Consult your lawyer about the Bulk Sales Act as it applies to your own situation. In some cases there are alternatives to direct compliance such as the seller's paying off all creditors before the closing, and signing a statement that there are no debts outstanding.

Finally, some states mandate that a seller secure a "certificate of good standing" from the state certifying that there are no known outstanding tax liabilities against the company. While a tax liability would technically be covered under the bulk sales provision, the state can demand such certification to give it an extra measure of protection. Obtaining certification can take longer than the 30 days generally required by the Bulk Sales Act. Check with your attorney about the regulations and the time requirements in your state in order to avoid delays in closing a sale.

Liens and Encumbrances

A bank or other lender or creditor of your target business may have placed a lien against property owned by the business, by the owner personally, or both. This means in essence that the encumbered property can't legally be sold without either paying the indebtedness or otherwise negotiating a release of the encumbrance with the creditor. Banks will often take out a blanket lien on all the property of a corporation to protect their position.

If you are not sure about whether there are encumbrances placed on the company (or associated property) that you are considering, check with the secretary of state's office in your state, and with the city or town in which the owner lives and the city or town where the target business is located. Your attorney can arrange to have a lien search performed and a report delivered to you.

While the cleanest way to get a lien removed is to pay the indebtedness, it may be possible to make other arrangements. For example, a lender might let you assume the lien and the responsibility for the debt upon closing. It is not unusual for a closing to take place with the seller immediately taking the proceeds from the sale and paying off indebtedness thereby releasing encumbrances.

Your lawyer and the seller's lawyer must decide how to remove any existing liens to assure that the business is acquired free and clear of encumbrances, or to decide on a strategy for transferring ownership with the new owner assuming the debt and the liens.

Offer to Purchase

When you are ready to make an offer, the seller or broker may ask you to present an *Offer to Purchase*. You will probably also be asked to include a check for a small percentage of the purchase price as *earnest money*. This offer will describe the price and terms under which the buyer will buy the business. The earnest money will usually be held in escrow while the offer is pending, and used as part of the purchase price if the offer turns into an actual purchase.

Your offer to purchase agreement can, and probably should, contain several contingencies such as review of financials by a CPA, physical count of inventory, proof of necessary licenses, and a stipulation that you are able to obtain financing at prevailing rates. You may add other contingencies that you deem necessary to your offer. The contingencies are basically escape mechanisms for you to withdraw from the deal under prescribed circumstances. A purchase and sale agreement (explained below) may also contain a number of contingencies, especially if there is no written offer to purchase agreement.

You should insist that your offer to purchase contain a deadline by which the seller must respond. If the seller does not respond by the stated deadline date, the offer is either automatically withdrawn, or withdrawn at your option. If the seller accepts the offer, he or she must stop looking for another deal while the accepted offer is pending. For this reason, a seller will want to impose his or her own deadlines for contingencies to be exercised and the deal to be finalized.

In some cases, the offer to purchase is skipped, and the buyer and seller proceed directly to the purchase and sale agreement.

A sample Offer to Purchase Agreement is contained in the Appendix.

Letter of Intent

For practical purposes, a letter of intent is the same thing as an offer to purchase. It states that an individual or entity intends to take a certain action (purchasing a company in whole or part) under a certain set of circumstances. Letters of intent tend to be used for transactions that have some complexity to them.

As with an offer to purchase, once a seller signs off on a letter of intent, he or she should stop all attempts to sell the business while the letter of intent is active.

Due Diligence

An offer to purchase or a letter of intent will generally include a contingency regarding verification. You (or your advisors) will have the right to examine the books, legal agreements, market data, and other information that is relevant to the company. This examination process is called the due diligence process. This means that you have the responsibility to exercise *due diligence* or appropriate care and caution, in investigating the seller's property, records, financial data, market data, etc.

The due diligence process must be carried out carefully. While it is the seller's responsibility to provide the information, it is your responsibility to examine and evaluate the information presented. If the seller provides the information without withholding damaging facts, and you do not properly evaluate the information, it will be very difficult for you to later initiate a claim of misrepresentation, after the business changes hands.

If, for example, a seller gives you 100 pages of documents during the due diligence process, and a page buried within details the fact that an important customer is going out of business, it is the your responsibility to review the information, and make a decision about whether or not to proceed. You will not be able to later sue the seller saying that he never pointed this fact out. The fact that he provided the document, even without drawing attention to it, is legally adequate.

The Contract (Purchase and Sale Agreement)

At the point where buyer and seller feel they have a deal (usually after an offer to purchase is accepted) a more complete contract, often called a purchase and sale agreement, must be drafted. However, don't rush off to your lawyer too early. The time to consult your lawyer is the point where most of the deal is worked out in plain English. Your lawyer can then advise you about some of the legal points and put the agreement into the proper language so that you are protected. If you bring your lawyer into the picture with many issues unresolved, your legal fees will be higher because he or she will have to spend more time on your behalf. Also, introducing additional parties to the negotiation introduces the risk of more arguments and perhaps frozen issues.

A contract, or purchase and sale agreement, will generally cover the following points:

(1) What is being sold?
(2) When is the buyer taking over the business? (closing date)
(3) The purchase price and (i) how and (ii) when it is to be paid.
(4) What security is the buyer is providing to the seller for any deferred payments that may be involved?
(5) Operation of the business during the interim between the signing a purchase and sale agreement and the closing.
(6) Non-compete agreement.
(7) Warranties by the seller to the buyer, as well as warranties by the buyer to the seller.
(8) Other adjustments.
(9) Contingencies.

Each of these points is addressed below:

- **What is Being Sold?**

To say you are buying a business is fine for casual conversation. From a legal perspective, though, it is not enough. Lawyers for both sides will insist that the tangible and intangible specifics of the transaction are spelled out in detail. Are you buying a corporation, or are you buying assets (see discussion above, stock versus assets sale)? If you are buying assets, which assets? What about the liabilities? Will you take them over, or will the seller be responsible for them?

Also the sale must be carefully allocated as discussed in Chapter XIV.

- **Closing Date**

In most situations, the buying of the business is a two-stage arrangement. First, the purchase and sale agreement is signed; second, the business is taken over on some subsequent date. One of the reasons for this two-stage arrangement is the need to take inventory. In a business that has inventory, this inventory changes from day to day even while you prepare for the sale. Most often you will agree to a price on the assumption that the inventory is at a certain level. The agreement should state the assumed level and state how the price will be adjusted if the level is different based on an actual count on closing day. In most cases, the buyer and seller agree to a price for the business, and they agree to a date on which the business will change hands. A lot of business closings take place on Monday so inventory can be taken over the preceding weekend.

- **Price — Payment Terms — Security**

As discussed in a number of areas in this book, price and terms for a business transaction can be a bit complex. There can be earn out provisions and other contingency payment arrangements that depend on future earnings or some type of agreed upon benchmark, seller financing, and employment contracts (for the seller) that must be detailed. Even a relatively straight forward all cash deal usually provides for some adjustments such as inventory and similar issues.

The contract will detail the method of payment. If it is a lump sum cash payment, the contract will state that. If it is an installment payment, the contract will have to provide for the period over which the installments have to be paid, the rate of interest, the form of the promissory note, the installment schedule, as well as the definition of the kind of security that you are pledging to the seller to guarantee the payments.

If part of the purchase price is to be paid in installments, the seller will want to get as much security as possible. That is, he will likely want to hold a security interest in all the assets of the business being sold, the furniture, fixtures, receivables, inventory, and so on. He may also want to secure the installments with other assets that you own, such as your home or another asset that you own. It is, of course, in your interest to pledge as little security as possible. In any case, the actual security stipulations must be agreed to and reduced to writing.

- **Operation of the Business between Contract and Closing**

Most contracts provide that the seller must maintain the status-quo of the business up until the closing. That is, the owner will agree to keep prices approximately the same, keep the inventory the same, maintain employment status, keep the same hours, and so on.

- **Non-compete Agreement (Covenant not to Compete)**

In nearly all cases, when you buy a company, you should insist that a seller agree not to compete with you for a minimum period of time. Generally, non-compete agreements are for two to five years. However, you must be careful in preparing the non-compete agreement. For a non-compete agreement to stand up in court, it usually must be significantly limited in scope. If, for example, a seller of a retail pet shop agrees not to compete in the retail pet industry anywhere in the U.S. for five years, a judge would probably rule the agreement too broad and invalidate it. Note that the court might not alter the agreement but might invalidate it completely, meaning that the seller would be free to compete with the business he sold, even to the extent of opening up right across the street. On the other hand, a nationwide non-compete agreement would probably be held valid if the business sold was national in scope.

A non-compete agreement limited in scope to the city or even the neighborhood where the pet shop is located is much more likely to be upheld by the court, and therefore is more valuable to you. However, it is usually not considered overly broad for a non-compete agreement to provide that the seller is not allowed to contact the customers of the business he sold, should the seller go into business outside the range provided in the agreement.

Don't fall for the trick some sellers use of offering a very broad non-compete agreement that they know can not be enforced. The rationale guiding non-compete agreements is that a person can not be overly restricted in his or her right to earn a living in a free market system. Seldom are non-compete agreements serious impediments to closing a deal.

Also, a non-compete agreement can provide a tax advantage to you in some instances. This is covered in detail in Chapter XIV.

- **Warranties**

For the most part, the warranties are those that the seller gives to the buyer. These typically include some or all of the following:

(1)   The seller has the right or authority to sell the business that he is selling.

(2)   The assets that the seller is selling are unencumbered by any liens or other such claims (see subsection above — Liens and Encumbrances).

(3)   The financial information, which was provided in writing to the buyer, fairly represents the financial situation of the seller.

(4)   There have been no major changes in the business since the financial documents were prepared.

(5)   The leases and other contracts that are being assigned to the buyer are in full force and effect.

(6)   There are no lawsuits or other litigation against the seller except those that have been disclosed, if any.

(7)   Any licenses or permits that are necessary for the business are in effect.

(8)   The equipment being sold is in good working order (except as specified).

(9)   The inventories are at a certain level, and that any deviation from the level will be adjusted at closing.

(10) The receivables are at the stated amount, and should they vary, they will be adjusted up or down at the closing.

As the buyer you will be asked to provide few warranties, if any. If you are asked for any warranties, the most likely one is that you will not use any information that you gained during the negotiations to compete with the seller or to the seller's detriment in any manner, should the deal collapse.

In practice, you will probably be asked to sign a non-disclosure agreement (also called *confidentiality agreement*) early on in the discussion phase. This agreement also states that you will not use any information gained to the seller's disadvantage.

• **Other Adjustments**

Items in this category are often the most difficult and quarrelsome. Some of the items of adjustment are rather straight-forward, such as utility and rent adjustments. That is, an adjustment is made for any utility bills that will have straddled the closing and therefore be incurred partly during the seller's ownership of the company, and partly during your ownership (after the closing). Likewise if rent is prepaid on the first of the month and the transaction closes on the tenth, you will owe the seller two-thirds of a month's rent, unless other arrangements are made.

Other items such as prepaid insurance and security deposits must also be adjusted. Also, adjustments for bills received after the closing that are shared responsibility must be adjusted.

Several other types of adjustments are a bit less straight-forward and warrant consideration and discussion. Let's look at three examples:

Example 1.

Assume that you are acquiring a business in June and that you are planning to retain the employees. Traditionally, in this particular business, vacations are taken in July and August. Some sort of adjustment may be needed to account for the fact that the vacations have been earned for work in the previous year, but the burden of paying for these vacations will now fall on you.

There can be different solutions for this, such as, money being set aside in escrow, or paid to the employees prior to the closing. This kind of issue and others like it must be discussed and settled in writing.

Example 2.

In this example, we'll assume that you are acquiring a going business, but you are not buying the receivables. Customer "X" owes money for previous purchases. After the closing he buys more goods and then sends in a partial payment. Should the payment be applied to the previous owner's receivables, to your own receivables, or should it be somehow divided? This kind of situation should be decided before closing the sale.

Example 3.

In this example, let's suppose you are buying a retail store that has a rather liberal policy of returns and exchanges. To retain the customers' goodwill, you decide to continue the liberal return policy. After the closing, several customers come in and ask to return goods. Who is going to be responsible for the refunds? Several solutions to this kind of issue are possible, but once again it all must be carefully thought out and agreed to in advance.

- **Contingencies**

Finally, a purchase and sale agreement might contain contingencies. That is, it may contain conditions that must be satisfied, or one party or the other (as specified in the agreement) may cancel the deal. For example, the deal may be contingent upon your being able to obtain appropriate financing, the seller providing updated financial information that demonstrates a specified level of performance, or a review of the firm's records. An offer to purchase agreement (if there is one) may also contain contingencies.

Attorney's Fees

Even for the purchase of a very small business, the legal expenses entailed in transacting it are substantial. It can easily cost a couple of thousand dollars to have the agreement(s) drawn, for advice along the way, and for the actual closing. The purchase and sale agreement is a major part of the expense. If the seller's lawyer draws that agreement, your legal bill will be lower, but it may be false economy. Many buyers feel that they will be better protected if their own lawyer draws the agreement.

Ask your lawyer about fees in advance to avoid unpleasant surprises. Lawyer's generally charge by the hour. The fact that the transaction is relatively small in dollar amount may not lessen the time required to prepare the required documents and attend the closing. It is proper to request a limit on fees.

Choosing An Attorney

If you already have an attorney with whom you are happy, who is familiar with small business transfers, by all means use that attorney. However, many fine lawyers with extensive experience in general law, do not have appropriate experience in this area. It is possible that your family attorney who has served you well for 15 years is not the best choice of a lawyer to assist you with buying your business. The attorney who negotiated a large settlement when you were hit by a car, is not necessarily the best choice for a business negotiation.

If you do not have an attorney that you trust, or if your trusted attorney is not versed in small business transfers, find an attorney who is experienced in this area. Don't be afraid to ask a prospective attorney if he or she has been involved in a number of such transactions before. A lawyer who does a lot of business transactions will not only have the experience to protect you, but will also be in a better position to get the work done quicker, and at less cost, simply because he or she will not need to spend as much billable time on your case.

XIV Tax Consequences

The manner in which the deal is structured will impact on your tax liability this year, and quite possibly for several years to come. Certain items involved in a business acquisition can be *expensed*; others must be depreciated over time, and some can not be deducted until the business is sold or otherwise disposed of. To some degree you (in consultation with your tax advisor) can minimize your tax liability, as we'll demonstrate below. Under current tax code, there is, on the other hand, not a lot that a seller can do to alter his tax liability from a business sale. Let's look at the seller's situation first.

Tax Liability — Seller's Perspective

Until 1986, capital gains, such as the gain an owner might receive on the sale of a business, were given advantageous treatment by the IRS. From 1986 to 1990, capital gains were given no special tax treatment; they were treated as ordinary income for tax purposes. Congress reinstated some special treatment for capital gains effective in 1991 by setting 28% as the maximum tax for such gains. However, because the top tax rate is only 3 points higher (31%), and because certain tax benefits are phased out for high income persons, the tax advantage of such gains is nearly inconsequential for most tax payers.

From the seller's perspective, only the time at which the money from the sale is received will have a major impact on tax liability. If the money is received over a number of years, it is taxed in the years received. This may not lower a seller's tax bill, but it will stretch out the due dates.

Also, the tax on the gain from a business sale is generally not due until April 15 of the year following the sale. For this reason, some sellers like to push late in the year closings into January. This way they can keep the money in an interest bearing account and not have to settle up with the government for up to fifteen months.

Understanding the seller's perspective may help you negotiate. For example, if changing the date of closing from December 19 to January 2 will cost you nothing but save the seller a few thousand dollars, it might be a painless concession to make.

Tax Liability — Buyer's Perspective

The way in which the sale is allocated can have a major impact on your tax bill That is, so much of the sale price is allocated for equipment, so much for inventory, employment or consulting contracts, and so much for goodwill.

Some parts of the sale price can be treated as business expense, and other parts can not. For example, a non-compete agreement can be expensed over the number of years for which it is in force. If it is a three year non-compete agreement, it can be expensed over three years, and so on.

Equipment and other tangible assets (not including inventory) can be depreciated using current IRS accelerated depreciation schedules. Goodwill, can not be depreciated. If you (as the buyer) later sell or liquidate the business, and there is a gain or loss in the value of goodwill, that will have to be recognized and dealt with at that time for tax purposes.

In order to best illustrate the importance of the allocation or "the deal-structure" and its tax consequences, let's look at four examples. These are examples only, and some of the techniques described may not be permissible in your situation. Seek the advice of your tax advisor before allocating an acquisition.

Case 1.

For this example we will assume that you are buying an employment agency where there are few if any tangible assets, and where you have agreed on a price of $60,000 for the business. Essentially what you are buying in this situation is 1) an agreement by the seller not to compete and 2) goodwill. In this case, there is considerable discretion as to how much is allocated to the non-compete agreement and how much to goodwill. Let's look at the two extreme options below. The first option allocates $10,000 to the non-compete agreement and $50,000 to goodwill. In the second option the situation is reversed; $50,000 is allocated to the non-compete agreement and $10,000 is allocated to goodwill.

	Option 1	Option 2
Non-Competition Agreement	$10,000	$50,000
Goodwill	$50,000	$10,000
Total Price	$60,000	$60,000

Option 2 is the better allocation choice. The reason is, that the non-compete agreement can be depreciated over its life. If we assume that the non-compete agreement will last for say two years, then you can write-off $25,000 each year- take it off the bottom line from a tax point of view over these two years. Under the scenario of Option 1, only $5,000 per year could be taken off your tax liability.

Case 2.

For this example assume that you are buying a clothing store. You are basically purchasing the customer base and inventory for a total price of $100,000. Let's assume that the seller is carrying the inventory on his books at the full price he paid of $90,000. However, the clothing business is fashion oriented, and the inventory will probably not retain its full value. If the seller tried to sell those same clothing items to a discount store, he would be lucky to get $20,000 for the whole lot. So here you are again faced with two possible options.

	Option 1	Option 2
Inventory	$ 90,000	$ 20,000
Goodwill	$ 10,000	$ 80,000
Total Price	$100,000	$100,000

Under Option 1 $90,000 is allocated for the inventory, and $10,000 for the goodwill. Under Option 2 $20,000 is allocated to the inventory and $80,000 to goodwill. Again, one option is far better than the other from a tax point of view. Here's why: Let's assume that after you acquire the business, you resell the clothing at retail and receive gross revenues of $150,000. Under the Option 1 scenario, your gross profit is $60,000 ($150,000 retail sales minus $90,000 for costs of goods = $60,000). Under the second option, gross profit is $130,000 ($150,000 revenue minus $20,000 in cost = $130,000). Let's further assume operating costs of $50,000 for both situations. Therefore your tax bill would be on profits of $10,000 in the first situation, but on $80,000 in the second situation. Obviously, there is very large difference in gross profit, and therefore in tax consequences.

Case 3.

Again, let's assume that you are buying a clothing store. This time, the agreed price is $65,000. In this case, you are not buying the inventory. What you are buying is the location, employees, and rights to the lease. The annual rent is just $20,000, whereas comparable space in the vicinity is going for over $35,000. Assume that there are four more years to go on the lease and therefore, taking over this lease gives you an advantage of $15,000 for each of the next four years.

Again, there are two possible options:

	Option 1	Option 2
Lease takeover	$ 60,000	0
Goodwill	$ 5,000	$ 65,000
Total Price	$ 65,000	$ 65,000

Under Option 1 $60,000 is allocated to the lease-takeover advantage (the financial value of taking over the lease) and $5,000 is allocated to goodwill. In option 2 everything is allocated to goodwill. Option 1 is the clear choice here for tax purposes. The lease advantage can be written off over the four years that the advantage is in effect. Under Option 2, no write off is allowed. Goodwill can be neither depreciated nor expensed under current tax law.

Case 4.

For the final example, let's assume that you are acquiring a manufacturing business. In essence, you are purchasing machinery and goodwill, for a total price of $100,000. This highly specialized machinery can last for many years provided that it is properly maintained. After investigating, you determine that if comparable used machinery were to be assembled, tested, outfitted, and placed in the proper position, it would cost $80,000. However, if this same machinery were sold piecemeal to a machinery broker, one would be fortunate to retrieve $30,000. So there are two allocation options. We could either appraise the machinery at the cost of putting it all together, or we could appraise it at what it would fetch if we were to sell it off on the second-hand market. Clearly, allocating the higher price for the machinery is more advantageous to the buyer:

	Option 1	Option 2
Machinery	$ 80,000	$ 30,000
Goodwill	$ 20,000	$ 70,000
Total Price	$ 100,000	$ 100,000

By allocating a higher value ($80,000) to the machinery, this equipment can probably be depreciated over the next ten years (or less) for tax purposes at a considerable tax advantage. Note that for tax purposes, this write-off can be taken even if the equipment remains useable beyond the depreciation period.

The above examples demonstrate that the less you can allocate to goodwill the better off you will be at tax time. In order to illustrate the point, we have offered simple examples with only one variable in each. In real transactions, it is common to have several variables that must be considered in allocating the sale for maximum tax advantage.

Allocation must be done correctly to pass muster with the IRS. The allocation must be defensible under tax regulations. For this reason, we recommend that you consult your tax advisor before finalizing an allocation in any buy/sell transaction. The money and time it takes will be money and time well spent.

Conclusion

For an individual, buying a going business can be a quicker and less risky entry into small business than either starting a company or buying a franchise. For an existing business, buying can be a low risk, low cost, and fast route to expansion.

However, finding and acquiring a company is not easy. Good acquisition candidates do not come along every day. A buyer must plan on devoting time and effort to finding a good acquisition target, and to evaluating that acquisition before purchasing it. Further, buying a firm is inherently dangerous to those not familiar with the process. You must be very careful and you should hire the right advisors to look over your shoulder to be sure that you are not unknowingly making a mistake.

However, the rewards of buying a company more than outweigh the difficulties and dangers entailed. It is an efficient path to small business profits for those with the patience and determination to do it correctly.

Appendix

The following is a sample valuation report that further demonstrates the excess earnings method of valuation. This report uses as an example the same fictional company (Harbor Locksmiths, Inc.) that was used to demonstrate the method in Chapter VII. However, this report differs slightly from the example in Chapter VII:

> The example in Chapter VII assumes that the business is bought including cash and receivables, and that the buyer takes over all liabilities. This example assumes that the seller retains cash and receivables; only specified assets are part of the transaction. Further, this example assumes that the seller retains responsibility for all liabilities. In the Chapter VII. example, the buyer assumed (took over) the liabilities.

> The Chapter VII example uses an interest rate of 11%. This example uses consumer price index plus 4 points which computes to about 9.4% as of this writing. This too will have an effect on the calculation. The logic of this method of computing cost of money is explained within the sample report.

The balance sheet and income statement referred to within the report are the same ones as contained in Chapter VII.

April 4, 1991

Mr. Irving Jones
44 McGrath Place
San Diego, CA 19200

Dear Mr. Jones:

Thank you for the opportunity to estimate the value of the company that you may purchase, Harbor Locksmiths, Inc.

There are a number of different methods that can be used to place an estimated value on a business. Different methods can yield different results. In fact, even the same method can yield different results because different appraisers will use different assumptions and different calculation procedures.

In valuing this company, we used the *excess earnings* method. We feel that this method offers a good estimate of value for small businesses that are earning money.

The excess earnings method of valuation uses the compensation being earned by the owner(s) of the business as the basis for valuation. It also adds in the fair market value for the assets owned by the business that will be included in the sale (such as equipment, inventory, etc.).

Based upon this method, we feel that a fair value for Harbor Locksmiths, Inc. is $356,622, if sold on a debt free basis. This valuation assumes that the only assets of the business that are included for valuation purposes are those being included in the sale. For example, if the business were to be sold using this valuation figure, the seller would keep all cash, accounts receivables and other assets not specifically included in this report. Responsibility for liabilities (up to the closing of the sale) would remain with the seller. This is how a business is typically sold when sold on an asset (not corporate stock) sale basis.

Here's how we came up with the number of $356,622:

We used the firm's gross sales figure of $508,115 for 1990. We then subtracted the cost of goods sold of $238,565. We also subtracted operating costs of $160,403.

gross sales	$ 508,115
cost of goods sold	$ 238,565
operating costs	$ 160,403

The way we came up with operating costs needs some explanation.

Operating costs as stated on the firm's income statement were $243,674. We deducted from this number (added back to profits) or added to this number (subtracted from profits) the following items:

depreciation	$ 1,786
owner salary	$ 80,000
interest expense	$ 4,800
miscellaneous adjustments	($ 3,315)
(see schedule of adjustments, attached)	
Total Adjustments	$ 83,271

The first three items (depreciation, owner salary, and interest) are explained later. The miscellaneous adjustments (sometimes called *add backs*) include monies spent by the business that are not absolutely necessary to the running of that business and therefore are considered as compensation to the owners. Items such as child day care, personal use of company vehicles, contributions, and retirement plans that are of benefit solely to the owners are typical adjustments or add backs. Conversely, it also includes adjustments for expenses that are lower than they will be for the new owner. An example of this is a rental expense or another expense that will be significantly increasing. The actual adjustments included for Harbor Locksmiths, Inc. are listed in the appendix to this report.

Depreciation and owner salary are treated as follows:

Depreciation

While Harbor Locksmiths, Inc. is reporting depreciation of $1,786, this is probably not an accurate reflection of the amount which the property owned by Harbor Locksmiths, Inc. decreases in value each year. Instead of this depreciation figure we calculated the amount of money that might be set aside in a special account to pay for eventual replacement of the business property being depreciated. The formula uses a one year contribution to this fund instead of the depreciation expense, as calculated for tax purposes. For this company we used 14% (approximately) of your estimate of fair market value of business equipment, furniture, and fixtures, and leasehold improvement.

Adjusted Depreciation Expense $800
(14% x $5,847 = $800)

Owner's Salary

We estimate that it would cost about $55,000 to hire a competent manager to run Harbor Locksmiths, Inc., if the owner were not working in the business for the number of hours that he is working. A fair market salary should be included as a business expense for buying and selling purposes. The reasoning is that in taking over the business, you will either have to pay a manager to run the company, or you will run it yourself. If you elect to run the business yourself, you should be paid a fair market salary for the time you spend in running the business, before any profits are calculated.

Adjusted Earnings Before Interest (And Taxes)

The adjusted earnings for the business before interest expense are calculated as follows:

gross sales	$ 508,115
cost of goods sold	$ 238,565
operating costs	$ 160,403
adjusted depreciation expense	$ 800
manager's salary	$ 55,000
Adjusted earnings before interest (and taxes)	$ 53,347

Tangible Assets Value

According to the information that you provided to us, the fair market value of the assets owned by the business are as follows:

inventory	$ 241,891
furniture and fixtures	$ 4,295
business equipment and other assets	$ 1,552
Total assets (real estate excluded)	$ 247,738
Total assets including real estate	$ 247,738

Note that if real estate is owned by the company, it is not included as part of this valuation. We feel that real estate should be valued and transacted separately for this kind of business. However, a fair market rent (or the rent actually being charged) must be included as an expense for valuation purposes because the buyer will have to pay that rent as a business expense.

All of the non-real estate tangible assets included in a sale are valued at their fair market value. However, buyer and seller often differ as to the fair market value of the assets.

Use of Money

The excess earnings method of valuation takes into account the fact that you will have to tie up some money in the business being bought. You may purchase the firm with your own cash, with borrowed money, or with some combination of the two. To borrow money, you will have to pay interest at a rate of 1% to 4% over prime. If you use your own money, an *opportunity cost* for the money must be considered. That is, you are passing up the opportunity of investing your money in any number of alternative investments and of earning a return in the form of interest, dividends, or both.

To put the cost of money on a level playing field, we use a number that disregards whether it is on a borrowed or opportunity cost basis. It considers instead the current cost of borrowing and current interest rates being paid by banks, the government, etc. The number, called the *underlying interest rate*, is based on the current rate of inflation. It is calculated by adding 4 points to the annualized increase in the consumer price index (CPI). This yields a number mid-way between estimated opportunity cost of a safe investment and borrowing cost at the prevailing rate for small business borrowing. The current CPI annualized increase as reported by the U.S. Department of Commerce is 5.4%, so the underlying interest rate is 9.4% (5.4% + 4 points).

This underlying interest rate is applied to the amount of money that needs to be tied up in working capital on a continuous basis. To approximate this amount, we used the net worth of this business (assets minus liabilities) as it is shown on the most recent balance sheet. In some situations this amount must be adjusted, to account for a net worth that is not in line with the needs of the business. For example, if the business is carrying too much cash on hand, or too much inventory for its needs, an adjustment was made. The adjusted amount is an estimate of the tangible net worth of the business that will be required, after the acquisition is completed (no adjustment was made in this particular situation).

adjusted net worth	$ 277,940
underlying interest rate	9.4%
cost of money	$ 26,126
(underlying interest rate) x (adjusted net worth)	

The cost of money figure of $26,126 is considered a business expense for Harbor Locksmiths, Inc. As noted above, this number is used *instead* of your actual interest expense.

Excess Earnings of Harbor Locksmiths, Inc.

The actual excess earnings of Harbor Locksmiths, Inc. for valuation purposes is the sales minus the expenses and minus the estimated amount that a manager would be paid (or that the owner should be paid as fair market salary):

gross sales	$ 508,115
cost of sales	$ 238,565
operating costs	$ 160,403
adjusted depreciation expense	$ 800
manager's salary	$ 55,000
cost of money	$ 26,126
excess earnings	$ 27,221

Earnings Multiplier

There are a number of factors that will have an impact upon the future of a business. The factors that we consider here for valuation purposes are competitiveness, the industry as a whole, risk, the performance of Harbor Locksmiths, Inc. relative to the industry, industry and company growth projections, and the desirability of the business. Each of these factors is rated on a scale of 1 to 6. A higher number means a better rating (6 is best and 1 is worst). Ratings are based upon the information that you provided, industry projections, industry performance statistics, and on our own judgment.

Here are the factors we used for Harbor Locksmiths, Inc..

Competitiveness   4.00
(based on information you provided, and
  our judgment)

Industry   3.00
(based on recent industry projections
  as reported by U.S. Department of Commerce)

Risk   5.00
(based on industry characteristics
  as reported by U.S. Department of Commerce,
  and our judgment)

Company   4.00
(based on comparing your financial
  performance to industry statistics from
  Robert Morris Associates, Internal
  Revenue Service, or both)

Growth   3.00
(based on recent industry projections
  as reported by U.S. Department of Commerce)

Desirability   5.00
(based on our judgment of the attractiveness
  and appeal of the industry)

Average factor   4.00
(average of above, used as multiplier)

This factor (4.00) is multiplied by the excess earnings figure $27,221 to place a value on the excess earnings of the business:

Average factor x Excess Earnings = Value of Excess Earnings

        4.00 x $27,221 = $108,884

The final step in this valuation process is to add the value of excess earnings to the fair market value of the tangible assets of the business. Based on the information that you provided, the fair market value of the assets of Harbor Locksmiths, Inc. that would be included with the business is $247,738:

value of excess earnings	$ 108,884
+	
value of tangible assets	$ 247,738
=	
Value of Business	$ 356,622

Conclusion

Based upon the information that you provided, and based upon our research and our judgment, a fair value for Harbor Locksmiths, Inc. is $356,622, as of 12/31/90. It is important to note that this is the estimated value on an asset sale basis whereby the only assets that are sold are those included in the fair market value of business assets that you reported to us (no cash, no accounts receivables, no other assets), and the company is delivered to you on a debt free basis (seller pays all liabilities).

Appendix To Report

Schedule of Adjustments (Add Backs)

Item	Value Adjusted	
Auto Expense	$ 5500	
Rent	($ 9615)	*
Contribution	$ 800	**
Total of Adjustments	($ 3315)	
(This is the same number in the report		
listed as "miscellaneous adjustments)		

* This adjustment was made to account for the slated increase in rent for the current year.

** Recorded as advertising. An $800 ad was placed in a charity yearbook.

Note: Other items were added back to profits, then adjusted and returned in adjusted form. These items include depreciation, interest expense, and owner's salary. These were discussed in detail within the report.

Business Plan Constructor

This is a business plan (or business summary) outline that can be used to create a basic business plan. This particular outline is designed specifically for acquiring a company and for presentation to a lender. The phrases in bold parenthesis are suggested section headings.

I. **Introduction:** Explain that you propose to purchase an existing business. Explain the type of business that it is, sales volume, and purchase price. Don't go into great financial detail here — that will come later.

II. **Business Summary:** Summarize what the target business sells and whom its customers are. Give a very brief history of the company. Explain growth and changes over the years. This section should be about two or three paragraphs.

III. **Acquisition Rationale:** In concise detail, answer the questions, "What are you buying?" That is, "What value are you receiving?" Define the advantages of buying this firm versus starting your own business of this type. If the target company has an extensive customer base, say so. If it has proprietary capabilities, describe them. If buying is simply cheaper than starting from scratch, don't be afraid to state that. See Chapter IV on reasons to buy a company.

IV. **Current Opportunity or Current Direction:** This section should outline what you plan to do with the business and why it will be successful. Include those elements that you do not plan to change and those that you do plan to change (if any). For example:

"We plan to increase sales by 20% each year for the next 3 years. These sales will come 80% from existing channels now used by the firm and 20% through new channels that we (the new owners) can exploit because of our industry contacts." "The product is well accepted in the marketplace. For this reason no product changes are planned." If you have specific expertise or experience that can enhance the company, note that here.

V. **Summary of Financial Needs:** For example: (a) We need new debt of X dollars. (b) We need X dollars in venture financing. (c) We plan to finance this plan through internal funding of $X. Note: If your plan doesn't need outside financing, this section can be excluded.

VI. **Management:** Simply state the key people who are managing the business now, and who will be managing the business after the acquisition is completed.

VIa. **Experience of Management:** Provide some details about the backgrounds and accomplishments of the new management personnel. As appropriate, highlight education, business experience, business successes, or whatever else will help convince the reader of management's ability to successfully run this business. A current resume for key managers can be added as an appendix.

VII. **Business Goals:** This section should detail exactly what you want to achieve. For example, if your goal is to sell the business at a profit in five years, say so. If the goal is to double sales, or double owner's salary, or increase market share, say so here. It is important to have a clear goal to help in making decisions along the way.

It is a good idea to establish and clearly state (1) short term goals (less than 1 year), (2) medium term goals (1 to 3 years) and (3) and long term goals (3 years+).

VIII. **Target Market:** Explain whom the company is now selling to, and whom you intend to sell to after the acquisition. If you plan any changes here, explain why and how such changes will benefit the company. For a consumer market, define the characteristics of the target market in terms of demographics, lifestyle, geography, etc. The target market for snowmobiles, for example, might be: (1) upper income consumers, (2) sports and outdoor enthusiasts, (3) people living in or near areas that have a lot of snow, (4) people between the ages of 25 and 45.

For an industrial market, define the type of company on which the target company now concentrates. Also define who in the customer's company makes and influences the buy decisions.

The more hard data that you can include that proves the size and accessibility of your target market, the better. That is, prove your target market really exists and that you can get your message to them. The best proof, of course, is that the business has been marketing successfully for years to this market segment.

VIIIa. Market Niche: Small businesses almost always survive by serving a very specific market need. In this section, explain why companies buy the products or services of the target company, instead of from another company. Exactly what is it that the company is now offering your target market, and what will you offer them in the future? If you can improve upon the product or service (and plan to do so), explain that here. Explain the improvement from the customer's perspective *and* from the firm's perspective.

Also explain here — How does this business differ from other businesses in the same industry?

Warning: Lenders tend to be conservative. Don't paint this company to be too different from others in the industry.

VIIIb. Marketing Summary: Explain how services and products are marketed now, and any changes or expansions that are planned. Also, explain various marketing possibilities or alternatives that are being considered. Remember that an important advantage of buying versus starting is that systems and procedures, including marketing, are in place. Don't go overboard in marketing changes, especially at the beginning.

IX. Competition: Detail the target's competition here. For example: (1) Who are they? (2) Who is their market? (3) How do they operate? (4) What are their capabilities? (5) What is their size or estimated size? (6) Who are their customers?

IXa. Competitive Advantages: What advantages does the company have over its competition? Are there further advantages that you as the new owner can bring to the company?

IXb. Competitive Disadvantages: What advantages do (or might) competitors have? Don't avoid this section by saying that the competition has no advantages. Competition is a fact of life in a free market system. Realistically facing up to the competition helps you to better deal with it. It also convinces a financier that you are not being blind to tough business realities.

X. Potential Problems: If you are looking for any outside financing, it is important to *answer the negatives*. Lenders and venture capitalists are very accustomed to over optimistic entrepreneurs. If you don't find the potential problems, you can be sure they will. If you find them, the impact will be less severe because you will be in a better position to explain the solutions and mitigating circumstances if you have the luxury of advance preparation.

Xa. Problem Solutions and/or Mitigating Factors: Explain what you will do to minimize the impact of the above problems; how will you defend against them? Also, explain how the extent of the damage can be minimized if the potential problems do become reality.

XI. **Financial Statements:** Include the company's financial statements, the most current one first, then the two previous years. Or, put the statements into comparative form so that the current year is on the same page with each of the last three years.

XIa. **Recast Financial Statements:** Show the financial statements adjusted to give a truer picture of expenses and owner compensation after the transition in ownership. See the financial statements with adjustments in Chapter VII.

XII. **Acquisition Expenses & Initial Investment:** Detail the expenses entailed in acquiring the company. Include not only purchase price but also transaction costs such as attorney fees, closing fees, and broker fees (if paid by buyer). If you plan any upfront investment, detail that investment here. Also, if you plan to raise cash by selling any of the acquired assets, detail that here.

XIII. **Financial Projections:** Financial projections for each of the three years following the acquisition should be included here. This should include a cash flow statement broken down by month for the first year. It is advisable to have your accountant prepare these statements, or to at least to look over your work before presenting the plan to a lender or investor.

Sample Legal Forms

The following are sample legal forms used in buying a business. The forms included are: (1) a Confidentiality Agreement and an (2) an Offer To Purchase.

Caution: These forms are meant to assist the buyer and seller in the proposed purchase of a business. These forms are meant as sample guides only, and should be used for informational purposes only in the drafting of your own documents. Prior to use these and all other legal documents should be reviewed by your attorney to determine whether the same comply with all applicable state and federal laws.

Confidentiality Agreement

In connection with the possible acquisition by you or your company of _____ _____ (name of company), we will be furnishing you information regarding this business, its financial condition, and customers of the company. In consideration of obtaining this proprietary information, you agree that:

1. All the proprietary information furnished to you will be confidential.

2. Unless we agree otherwise in writing, you will not disclose or reveal any proprietary information for three years from this date to any person(s) or entity(s) other than your employees or representatives or advisors who are directly participating in the evaluation of this information for any purpose other than in connection with a proposed acquisition. Furthermore, you agree not to use any furnished information for your own benefit, for the benefit of any third party, or to the detriment of the seller.

3. If you decide that you do not wish to pursue the proposed acquisition, you will advise us of this fact and return all proprietary information furnished to you without keeping copies of it.

4. Although you understand that we have included in this proprietary information certain information which we consider to be relevant for the purpose of your investigation, we do not make any representation or warranty as to its accuracy or completeness.

If you are in agreement, please complete this form and indicate your acceptance by signing below.

Agreed to and accepted:

_____   _____
Signature   Date

_____   _____
City/State   Zip Code

_____   _____
Name (please print)   Address

_____   _____
Witness Signature   Date

Offer To Purchase

I,_____ as _____
           (Name)   (Title if applicable)

of_____ make the following offer to purchase
    (Name of company that is buying, if applicable)

_____. _____ will
     (Name of company being sold)   (Person or company making offer)

pay $_____ for the assets of the company including:

_____   _____

_____   _____

The amount will be paid as follows:

$_____ today as a good faith deposit and down payment; $_____ on _____
                                                                            (Date)

as an additional down payment; $_____ upon closing of the sale which is tentatively

scheduled for_____. $_____ over a period of _____
           (Date)

paid under the following schedule and terms:

_____

_____

The offer is contingent upon the following:

_____

_____

_____

In the event that such contingencies are not met by_____(Date), this offer may, at the buyer's option, be cancelled, and the deposit returned in full. If the buyer does not notify seller by this date to the contrary, all contingencies will be deemed waived.

If seller does not accept this offer by _____, it shall be deemed cancelled.

This offer is made on _____ by _____.
                          (Date)   (Buyer's signature)

Accepted by:

_____   _____
    (Seller's name and title)   (Seller's company)

_____   _____
    (Seller's signature)   (Date)

Bibliography

Business Valuation

Desmond, Glenn and Marcello, *John A. Handbook of Small Business Valuation Formulas.* Valuation Press, Inc. Marina Del Rey, CA, 1988. (A guide of rule of thumb formulas).

Desmond, Glenn and Kelley, Richard. *Business Valuation Handbook.* Valuation Press. Los Angeles, CA, 1980.

Pratt, Shannon. *Valuing Small Businesses and Professional Practices.* Dow Jones-Irwin. Homewood, IL, 1986. (An in-depth guide to valuation with details on each approach).

Buying and Selling Businesses

Goldstein, Arnold S. *The Complete Guide To Buying And Selling A Business.* New American Library. New York, NY, 1983.

Mancuso, Joseph, R., and Germann, Douglas D. *Buying A Business For Very Little Cash.* Prentice Hall Press. Englewood Cliffs, NJ,1990.

Schine, Gary L. *How To Sell Your Business For More Money.* The Consultant Press. New York, NY, 1991.

Industry Financial Data

Private Sources

RMA Annual Statement Studies. Robert Morris Associates, P.O. Box 8500, S 1140, Philadelphia, PA 19178 (215) 665-2850. (This is the best known and most commonly used guide to industry financial data) (updated annually)

Troy, Leo, *Almanac of Business and Industrial Financial Ratios.* Prentice Hall, Englewood Cliffs, NJ, 1988. (updated periodically)

Government Sources

Business Statistics 1961-1988. U.S. Department of Commerce- Bureau of Economic Analysis, U.S. Government Printing Office, Washington, DC. (This is a summary supplement to the Survey of Current Business (see next listing). It enables one to easily compare historical industry performance. It's useful in determining how an industry performed in previous economic recessions and expansions.)

Survey of Current Business. U.S. Department of Commerce-Bureau of Economic Analysis, U.S. Government Printing Office, Washington, DC. (Published monthly, this publication provides statistics on the economy as a whole, and on many specific industries.)

Corporation Source Book. The Statistics of Income Division of the Internal Revenue Service. Available for $175 from: Director, Statistics of Income Division, Internal Revenue Service, 1111 Constitution Avenue N.W., Washington, DC 20224. (Periodically updated, it is also available by specific industry for $1.00 per page.)

Partnership Source Book. The Statistics of Income Division of the Internal Revenue Service, Available for $30 from: Director, Statistics of Income Division, Internal Revenue Service. 1111 Constitution Avenue N.W., Washington, DC 20224. (periodically updated)

Sole Proprietorship Source Book. The Statistics of Income Division of the Internal Revenue Service. Available for $95 from: Director, Statistics of Income Division, Internal Revenue Service, 1111 Constitution Avenue N.W., Washington, DC 20224. (periodically updated)

Note that the preceding 3 IRS source books provide detailed breakdowns of industry financial averages and ratios, compiled from business tax returns. They are not currently available from the Government Printing Office.

Statistics of Income, Corporation Income Tax Returns, Publication Number 16. Internal Revenue Service, U.S. Government Printing Office, Washington, DC. 20402 (periodically updated)

Industry Projections

To find out how the industry you are considering buying into is projected to perform check out one or more of the following:

Predicasts Forecasts. Cleveland Predicasts, Inc. Cleveland, OH. (updated quarterly)

Standard and Poors Industry Surveys. Standard and Poors Corporations. New York, NY (updated regularly)

U.S. Industrial Outlook. U.S Department of Commerce, U.S. Government Printing Office, Washington, D.C. 20402. (An easy to read outlook on the prospect of over 350 different industries) (updated annually)

Note that some of the larger full service stock brokerage firms regularly publish industry survey and projection data that is available to the public.

Business Plans

Bangs, David H. *The Business Planning Guide.* Upstart Publishing Company. Portsmouth, NH, 1988.

Mancuso, Joseph R. *How To Prepare and Present a Business Plan.* Prentice Hall. Englewood Cliffs, NJ, 1983.

Rich, Stanley R. and Gumpert, David E., *Business Plans That Win $$$.* Harper and Row. New York, NY, 1985.

Other Reference Publications

Rates and other details on most U.S. periodicals that accept advertising (to search for businesses for sale by specific industry):

Business Publications Rates and Data. Standard Rate and Data Service. Wilmette, IL (monthly).

For a listing of companies in the direct mail list business:

Direct Mail Lists Rates and Data. Standard Rate and Data Service. Wilmette, IL (bi-monthly).

For a description, including address and phone number, of virtually every membership organization in the U.S.:

Encyclopedia of Associations. Gale Research, Detroit, MI (published annually).

For general information and sources of detailed information on a number of industries dominated by small business:

Small Business Source Book. Gale Research. Detroit, MI (revised periodically).

For a comprehensive guide to information and services available from the U.S. Government:

Lesko, Matthew. *Information U.S.A.* Viking and Penguin Books. New York, NY, 1986.

For information on labor, such as pay rates, projections for supply versus demand by field, etc.
Occupations Outlook Handbook. U.S. Department of Labor Statistics, Available from: Superintendent of Documents, U.S. Government Printing Office. Washington, DC. 20402 (updated annually).

Occupations Outlook Quarterly. U.S. Department of Labor Statistics, U.S. Government Printing Office. Washington, DC 20402 (updated quarterly).

Occupation Projection and Training Data. U.S. Department of Labor Statistics. U.S. Government Printing Office. Washington, DC 20402 (This title contains supply and demand forecasts for various occupations) (updated biannually).

Note: Publications listing the U.S. Government Printing Office as publisher are available from the U.S. Government Printing Office Superintendent of Documents, Washington, DC 20402-9325, (202) 783-3238.

Index